P9-DDE-231

A Sunset Book

OUTDOOR LIGHTING

BY THE SUNSET EDITORIAL STAFF

Editor for this book: Bob Horne

Lane Books · Menlo Park, California

Acknowledgments

In a field such as residential outdoor lighting, which, in a sense, is relatively new, our thanks and gratitude must be extended to many people who made their lighting installations available for photographing, and to the following people who contributed advice and designs for outdoor lighting and landscape illumination: John Watson, landscape illuminator, Dallas, Texas; Kathryn Stedman, landscape architect, Palo Alto, California; John Carmack, landscape architect, San Francisco; Ralph DeGarmo, Casella Lighting, San Francisco; Paul McMullen, landscape consultant, Los Gatos, California; Nancy Evans, residential lighting specialist, General Electric Company; Elizabeth A. Meehan, color and lighting design coordinator, Sylvania Lighting Center; Rita M. Harrold, director, residential lighting, Westinghouse Electric Corporation; May Love Gale, home economist, Tennessee Valley Authority; Milton C. Very, Hadco Products, Inc.; Humphrey Lee, Corolite; Frederick Locklin, Loran, Inc.; Walt Perram, Arizona Public Service Company; Darrel Haye, Kim Lighting, Inc.; Richard Larson, Pacific Gas and Electric Company, San Francisco; Ruby Redford, editor, Illuminating Engineering; and, Don Townsend, Cupertino Nursery, Inc., Cupertino, California.

Art illustrations throughout the book are the work of Sophie Porter, San Francisco, California.

The small garden shown on the cover was photographed at General Electric's Nela Park in Cleveland, Ohio. Detailed information on the lighting installation shown is found on pages 34–35. The architect is Fred Toguchi, Cleveland, Ohio. Photo courtesy of General Electric Company.

Fourth Printing March 1971
All rights reserved throughout the world. First Edition. Copyright © 1969 by Lane Magazine & Book Company, Menlo Park, California. Library of Congress Catalog Card Number 69-13275. SBN Title Number 376-01191-2. Lithographed in the United States.

CONTENTS

A blend of lighting from the interior of the home to the patio area creates a level of illumination that allows relaxation and enjoyment in the total living space of the home and surrounding area.

INTRODUCTION

Light has been controlled and fashioned by man for over 500,000 years. Uncontrolled and unpredictable light fashioned by nature has been around ever since primeval darkness was first penetrated by the sun.

The sun and moon and lightning were man's first exposure to outdoor lighting. He traveled the earth by day in the brilliance of the sun. At night, he rested and awaited the dawn. The pattern of man's life remained much the same for thousands of years. While the hazards of the day were fearsome, night brought terror; the unseen was the unknown. Frequent flashes of lightning followed by rumblings of thunder did little to dispel fear.

It is believed that lightning provided man with his first weapon against darkness—fire. Although fire was caused by accident, man recognized that fire as a source of light and heat could be controlled to meet his needs. By carrying coals and burning branches, man was able to take the fire to his cave, clearing, or encampment. It changed his way of life—he could dispel some of the terrors of the night.

With the change came a form of socializing—a gathering about the campfire for feasting and story telling. Perhaps fire did not create communications, but it certainly enhanced them. And it probably played a great part in stimulating the imagination and promoting camaraderie, for to this day there is something fascinating about looking upon burning logs on a hearth or in a fire pit.

Man learned to carry torches and to place them in holders along the cave or dwelling wall. Such lighting is still acceptable today for creating a mood outside by the barbecue or in the garden.

The history and development of man nearly parallels the development of methods of lighting from oil lamps, kerosene lanterns, and gas to electricity. All are ways to extend man's activities over a longer period.

And yet, many people still curtail their activities outside their home when night falls, rather than attempt to extend the usable hours on their property with outdoor lighting.

If this book does nothing else for you but increase the hours that you can use outdoor areas at night, it will more than pay its way by bringing a new dimension to living.

It is impossible to utilize your property to its fullest extent without outdoor lighting. The many lighting fixtures on the market today are designed to produce a variety of lighting schemes, and with a small amount of effort, substantial dividends can be realized. Not only will your property be more useful and attractive, but it will also be more valuable. Money spent on lighting can easily bring greater returns in enjoyment and in the resale value of your home.

LIGHT IS EMOTIONAL, TOO

Satisfying physical needs with lighting around the home and in the garden is, in itself, not enough. How you and your guests react to lighted surroundings is equally important. All varieties of lighting affect mood and emotion. Lighted landscaping harbors secrets and surprises; it can never be completely discovered.

Lighting will challenge your creativity. It is completely individualistic and allows you to be selective. The sun illumes all within view, but lighting at night can be both selective and creative.

It is the intention of this book to offer aid in lighting the outdoor areas around your home in both useful and attractive ways. Every home needs some outdoor lighting. It might as well be lighting that is in good taste—lighting that complements the beauty of your home.

To this end, the book is divided into sections that represent areas around the home to be lighted. Not only is there a need for good outdoor lighting, but it is also possible to have fun with light. For this reason, this book includes special sections on holiday lighting and party lighting. In keeping with the times, security lighting is also included to indicate that lighting that alleviates worry can also be attractive and relatively inexpensive.

To compile the information and photographs for this book, extensive field trips were taken and leading authorities in the field of outdoor lighting were interviewed. As landscape lighting borders on an art form, many different approaches to lighting were found. One fact stands out—there is no single approach to lighting. Guidelines are delineated to assist a person in lighting his property, but the actual lighting of an area around the home depends so much on the individual use to be made of the area and the effect to be created that considerable experimentation within the guidelines is recommended.

Lighting from attractive fixtures complements the architecture of the home.

NEED FOR LIGHTING

Total living with illumination

Every neighborhood has a character of its own. Drive along any residential street, and the mood and character of the homes that line each side will make an impression. Each property will have its differences, but it is the total effect rather than the individual difference that is felt.

Some neighborhoods attract, some repel, and some are strangely neutral. The same feelings are created at night, sometimes by the street lighting, or large shadowy trees, the warmth of lighting in entryways, or the quietude observed through the lighted windows of homes.

Harsh lighting effects at night stand out as plainly as does an overgrown lawn in the daylight, with one subtle difference. Residents on the street may know why the lawn at a particular house is overgrown, and, while they may not like it, they may accept it for one

reason or another. But harsh lighting at an entry or on a post by the drive may not even be noticed by the residents. Their eyes have been trained to see the neighborhood in a particular manner, and it is instead the occasional visitor to the neighborhood who notices these things most quickly. It is a peculiarity that our eyes see largely what they want to see, particularly in familiar surroundings.

But if one evening a new light post appears on a lawn where there had been no light before, attention is immediately drawn to it. A familiar pattern has been broken. If the effect is pleasing, other light posts of somewhat similar nature may appear along the street.

Perhaps one reason why ideas in lighting do not spread rapidly is that people are reluctant to change a familiar setting. In reality they do not "see" a familiar scene. They have learned to adjust to it, and with

their minds on a myriad of other things, they are reasonably content to leave their surroundings alone. Settled neighborhoods resist change more than new neighborhoods and new developments.

But people are inundated with ideas for home improvement. They see them in almost every magazine and newspaper. Slowly some of the ideas catch on, and when people look for a new home they are extremely conscious of the latest in home improvements and want as many of them as their money will reasonably allow. Even in settled neighborhoods, people are thinking of ways in which they can improve their home and property.

The degree of emphasis on improving the property surrounding the home is largely determined by the kind of neighborhood, the image to be reflected by the home, and the use to be made of the property. Ideally, the attractiveness wanted for the home is total—from the extreme front of the property to the back lot line.

For most people there is no magic wand that can be waved—presto—to make their entire domain as attractive as they would like it to be. Improving the property is generally approached one project at a time —a patio, a garden area, a barbecue, a fireplace, or whatever. In general, it is best to start with a simple lighting project—a single shrub, or steps and a walk way.

Lighting the outdoor areas of your home can be approached in much the same way—a portion at a time. Every home needs some outdoor lighting, and the attractiveness of your home should not be diminished at night with improper, glare-producing lights. Proper lighting of the premises offers hours of extra enjoyment and enhances the beauty of the home.

HOW TO VISUALIZE NIGHT LIGHTING EFFECTS

In one way or another, a lifetime can be spent training the eye to "see." One philosopher said it briefly: "What you see is what you are." Samuel Johnson, writing on foreign travel, said, in effect, that knowledge gained from travel is directly related to the amount of knowledge a traveller takes to a foreign country.

If, for example, you are familiar with the history, customs, and art of a country that you are traveling to, chances are you will "see" more of that country than will someone who has read only a colorful brochure. An experienced businessman will "see" more of the economic structure of a country than will a young student. In other words, the ability to relate knowledge to a new situation often produces the most satisfactory results.

Approaching outdoor lighting is no different. A person having a background in photography, stage lighting, and landscaping will master quite quickly the techniques and artistry of outdoor lighting, particularly lighting in the garden. But there are few people who have the advantages of such a background.

You can overcome the lack of a background in approaching outdoor lighting by training the eye to "see." Everyone has had an opportunity to see photographs in their own family album or in magazines, newspapers, books, and friends' snapshot collections. Some pictures are dull, some are interesting, and some even invoke enthusiasm. Instead of merely looking at and reacting to photographs, take the time to study some of them. Why are some interesting and some not?

Composing a light scene

A good picture will always have good composition and a feature of dominant interest. The eye senses the composition and travels to the dominant interest in the picture. But there is usually more. Continued examination of the picture may reveal areas of secondary interest, or tertiary, and so on. In one sense, the eye "feasts" on a good picture. Interest is sustained beyond a mere glance.

Almost everyone at one time or another has taken a photograph that is pleasing. By examining the "why," the eye is being trained to see. If they relate this to outdoor lighting in the garden, most people will be able to achieve pleasing lighting effects, after some experimentation and effort.

For a beginning, turn all the lights on inside the house. Go outside and take a look. Walk down the sidewalk and view your home and premises from varying distances and angles. Chances are you will be pleased with the effect—the warm light coming through the windows and spilling out onto the lawn, shrubs, and walks. Possibly, now that you are looking specifically at the lighting effects, some areas may be revealed that are not as pleasing as you would like them to be. Some remedies may come immediately to mind.

Turn on the house lights, please

Now, turn on all the lights on the outside of the house—entryway, garage, or whatever areas can be lighted. This is the total illuminated effect of your home. In many cases, your home will not look as attractive with the exterior lights on as it did with only the interior lights. One reason for this could be that outside lighting is thought of only in functional terms instead of the over-all effect that is created. The light on the garage over the driveway was put there for functional reasons—loading the trunk, changing a tire, or doing minor work on the car or power mower. The light in back may have been installed primarily so that it was easier to find the garbage cans or so that you could perform some late work on the back lawn or garden. In other words, you have a switch to flick to produce *necessary* light, then flick off when the need for lighting is over.

By stepping away from the house and looking at the lighting from a purely aesthetic sense rather than for its functional use, it is possible to see your home much as it would be seen by a visitor. Such objectivity is relatively easy to acquire once you start asking different questions of your eye.

Look not only at the home, but get back far enough to take a broader look at the neighborhood. Any lighting that is changed or added should be in character with the neighborhood. Lighting, like many other things, is a matter of relativity. An extremely well lighted entry could still be at too high a level for the neighborhood and, while attractive at the house, could be very unattractive in a neighborhood sense by its conspicuousness.

Keeping in mind the neighborhood, the potential attractiveness of your home, and the lighting needs of the property, make a check list, such as the following:

Entryway	Garage
Driveway	Patio area
Walks	Garden
Steps	Activity areas

Such a list will help in reviewing the entire lighting system from a need or utilitarian approach. It is not likely that the entire outdoor lighting program will be done at one time, but it is helpful to plan the goal and work toward it.

AREAS TO CONSIDER FOR NIGHT LIGHTING

ACTIVITY AREA
(Pg. 20)

GARDEN
(Pg. 28)

POOL (Pg. 24)

WALKWAY
(Pg. 18)

STEPS (Pg. 18)

PATIO (Pg. 14)

DRIVEWAY (Pg. 18)

ENTRYWAY
(Pg. 10)

Enter...as a Guest

What does your entry say?

Light and shadow create an inviting entryway. A good first impression of the home is established and guests can find their way easily and safely to the entry. Landscape Illuminator: John Watson of Dallas, Texas.

Guests looking for your home ordinarily recognize it by its lighted entryway. If they have never been there before they will look for the number there unless it is plainly lighted or designated elsewhere in the front of the house.

Entryways come in all shapes and sizes, but they all encompass a door—the entrance to the home. They all have one kind of light or another.

You should approach your own entry as a guest who has never been to your home before. This is not entirely realistic, but it will help form an idea of what the entryway actually says. If there are steps to the entry, make a special effort to see if they are easily identified. You know they are there, but a guest might not unless they are pointed out or well lighted.

Is the inherent beauty of an ornate fixture in the entryway entirely lost in the glare of a bright bulb?

You may have taken great care in selecting the door, for its design or, perhaps, for its unusual texture. Is its beauty lost in the flat, uninteresting lighting?

Are there plantings in the entry that could add interesting shadows or make attractive silhouettes with a small amount of additional lighting?

Lighting in the entryway to be most effective should be both functional and attractive. Specifically, the entryway lighting serves a transitional function of allowing guests to move safely and comfortably from the night into the bright indoors of the home without encountering annoying glare.

It is good to utilize architectural features of the entryway when considering the kind of lighting that is most suitable. Fixtures mounted on the wall may not be necessary if sufficient light spills from the doorway or adjacent windows, but in such event it is good to consider accent lighting from above or below to provide contrast to the flatness of effect from inside lighting.

Consider also that people leaving the house pass through the entryway, and any lighting should be positioned so that glare is not encountered in either direction.

An entryway can be an all-encompassing concept. Entry lighting can include post-type lighting located at the juncture of the sidewalk and entry walk, or lights under the eave or in the soffit to light the walkway to the entry. Small mushroom low voltage lights can also serve to light the walkway to the entry. In some instances, the driveway blends with the walk to the entry, and consideration should be given to making the lighting adequate from the drive to the entryway.

Whatever the lighting, it will be most enjoyed when it is both purposeful and attractive so that it is integrated with the lighting inside the home and blends well with the character of the neighborhood.

A good level of illumination is provided by combined lighting from overhead lights and outside fixture.

Lighting leads the way to interesting entryway with the interior lights blending with the outdoor lighting.

Light reflected from the adjacent wall is utilized to provide adequate illumination of walkway to entry.

Entryways are as individualistic as the homes they grace, and any fixtures chosen should help maintain the individualism. Small lighting fixtures are out of place in a spacious entry, and the use of higher wattage bulbs in small fixtures tends to accentuate the disproportionate relationship while, at the same time, unwanted glare is produced.

Interesting features of the entry can be emphasized with lighting. The door may have an unusual surface that produces attractive shadows and lines when grazed with light from above or to one side. Illumination of a brick wall may bring out interesting patterns that are not noticeable during the day. Or the silhouette of a container planting can be revealed effectively against the smooth surface of wooden siding.

In some entryways, the amount of lighting depends upon the level of illumination reaching the entry from the interior of the house, and whether or not the interior illumination is ordinarily cut off by drawn draperies or closed shutters.

One level of lighting may be desired for everyday use in the entry, while a higher level may be utilized when guests are expected. For this flexibility, appropriate switching and a dimmer should be located near the door.

But, whatever the lighting arrangement, keep in mind the attractiveness and the safety at your entry.

Suspended lighting fixture at entryway is proportioned to complement the architectural styling of the house.

Entry court provides a pleasant view from several rooms and is particularly suited for night lighting.

Massive wooden door offers interest when lighted from above. Good level of illumination at the entry step.

A bright bulb in the lighting fixture does not keep this entry from being dark, uninviting. Glare from the fixture obscures its attractive design, while the home's architectural beauty is lost in darkness. Note improvement below.

Illumination level has been reduced at the entry lighting fixture so that its design can now be appreciated. Additional lighting has been installed in the planter beds to reveal the beauty of the home.

Lighting the Patio

The room that is a view

A festive note is added to the patio by hanging stars from the cedar. Landscape Illuminator: John Watson.

Some confusion may exist as to the definition of a patio, but it is generally accepted to think of a patio as an outdoor room—a room that is more oriented to the out-of-doors than to the house, even though it might be structurally integrated with the house. In another sense, a patio can be a transition area between indoor and outdoor living, but the predominant emphasis on the patio is that of relaxation and pleasure, coming largely from the patio's out-of-door environment.

When it comes to lighting a patio, its difference from a room is readily apparent—there are few if any walls for reflecting light and often no ceiling surface. Such lack of reflecting surfaces, however, can be an advantage in that there is complete freedom in creating the desired mood and atmosphere entirely with lighting.

Each family must determine the use, or variety of uses, to be made of the patio and keep it in mind when selecting the lighting. In general, however, relaxation and a feeling of the outdoors is the most common approach to take regarding a patio. A relaxing mood is established by the softness of the lighting. But while a low wattage bulb that spreads light over the entire patio may give the effect of a soft light, it might not be attractive or interesting lighting. Rather, it might tend to be flat, and most likely someone will end up sitting so that the full wattage of the bulb strikes him directly in the eyes.

Lighting level for relaxation is not too critical. Sufficient luminosity is required to allow people to see one another and to light the patio furniture to prevent stumbling and collisions in the dark. Sometimes this kind of lighting can be achieved by overhead floodlamps. But, again, the flatness of overhead floodlighting should be countered with accent lights to afford contrast and interest. The addition of a dimmer switch can help control and vary the intensity of the lighting to add interest or to provide more light for parties and dining on the patio than would be required for mere relaxation and conversation.

A soft moonlight effect on the patio provides an ideal level of illumination for conversation and relaxation. Lighting the surrounding area enhances view. Landscape Illuminator: John Watson.

Numerous hanging and wall-mounted fixtures are available for patio lighting in both standard and low voltages. The over-all lighting effect in the patio is best when it is compatible with lighting available from within the house and any lighting elsewhere in the garden.

Another aspect of patio lighting to consider is the view of the patio as seen from the living room, family room, or wherever there is an interior room with a large window or sliding glass door opening onto the patio. The lighting should be of an intensity that can be viewed comfortably from within the home. Such attractive lighting on the patio in effect creates the illusion of enlarging the room connected to the patio, and such lighting also reduces glare from interior lights reflected on the glass surfaces.

Patio lighting is susceptible to numerous approaches. If the patio is more of a terrace that is elevated from an adjoining garden area, the view at night may be enhanced by lights mounted beneath the patio and directed toward the garden area.

Downlighting from the tree produces interesting light and shadow patterns on the patio and lawn.

The patio and garden are viewed from the interior of the home with the sliding glass door open on the left side. This daylight view of the patio and garden can be compared with the night view below.

With the sliding glass door remaining open on the left, it is possible to observe that the night lighting has removed reflections from the glass area on the right. All but one of the lights are beyond the wall.

Soft lighting on this attractive terrace makes it an inviting location for entertaining and relaxation.

Light shining into overhanging trees glows through spaces between laths to light patio.

Lighting effect tends to bring the patio-garden area closer to the house. Design: Sim Bruce Richards.

Walkways & Steps

Safety combined with attractiveness

Lighting beside the steps accentuates stone surface and improves visibility at the steps for safety.

There is some kind of path to every home, and every home has at least as many paths as it has entry doors. All of these doors that are used at night should have sufficient lighting. Perhaps the lighting requirements for areas used only by the family need not be as great as for those used by visitors or guests, but the lighting should be considered for all users of the paths about the home.

Among considerations to be made are the surface material of the walk, the reflectance of nearby walls or fences, and whether or not fixtures will be mounted on the ground or on nearby structures. Light-colored walls or fences and walkway surfaces usually will require less lighting than dark surfaces. The foliage or plantings near the walk must also be considered to determine the most effective height for lighting fixtures. Also, the lighting fixtures, whether close to the ground or mounted on the wall or fence, should be located so that glare is prevented.

The lighting of the paths and walkways, like other outdoor lighting, should be in unity with the lighting of the rest of the house and grounds.

When lighting steps, you must take care to avoid deep shadows at the wrong places. Some step lighting is off to one side, whereas other step lighting is built directly into the steps. In either event, glare should be eliminated so that the objective of safety is not defeated.

If the steps are lighted from overhead, care must be taken so that the shadow of a person walking up or down the steps does not interfere with the visibility at step level.

If plants or shrubs are near the light source, the patterns of light on the steps and walkways should be checked from time to time to determine that plant or shrub growth is not interfering with the light patterns or casting shadows that obscure the view.

Good walkway and step lighting is both functional and attractive, and, once installed, will add to the enjoyment of your property.

Aesthetic lighting can also be functional in allowing safe maneuvering of steps and walkways for people who are strolling outdoors during the late evening. Landscape Illuminator: John Watson.

Perspective of brick walkway is revealed with light highlighting the tree and background.

A light located beneath the steps can be an attractive way to illuminate open steps for safe passage.

Lighting Activity Areas

More fun with light

A shuffleboard court gives added pleasure when outdoor lighting is installed, permitting activities to continue during the evening hours. Lighting helps you to utilize your property to a greater extent.

Extending the use of your property for activities after dark is another advantage offered by outdoor lighting. Generally speaking, the level of illumination will be somewhat higher for activity areas than for areas meant only to be viewed. In general, the illumination level for most activities such as badminton, shuffleboard, tennis, basketball, and croquet will be on the order of 10 footcandles. For barbecues, picnics, and other outdoor lawn and garden activities, the level of illumination can be somewhat lower.

Again, the location of the lighting must be such that irritating glare does not extend to neighboring lots.

In lighting activity areas, the contemplated use of the areas must be considered as well as the amount of time that will be spent using such activity areas.

AREA LIGHTING GUIDELINES

Selecting area lighting equipment requires a combination of common sense, a technical appreciation of lighting, and a "feel" for the aesthetics of the lighting effect desired. No one set of rules will assure the best light for every situation. However, the following guidelines should be helpful.

1. Use mercury luminaires for 1000 burning hours per year or more. Filament lamps tend to burn out sooner.

2. Use the highest wattage bulbs and the fewest poles that will still deliver uniform lighting. Generally, spacing between poles should not exceed four times mounting height.

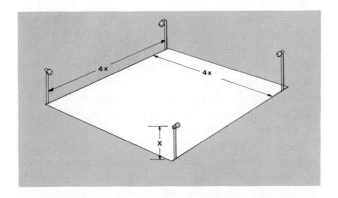

3. Use the widest beam spreads available, consistent with the good use of light.

4. Consider ease of re-lamping and occasional cleaning when selecting the lighting units.

5. The appearance of the lighting equipment—both day and night—is important.

An overhead floodlight allows a late evening game of basketball and provides garage area lighting.

A fast game of badminton requires good outdoor lighting after dusk. Keep glare from neighbor's property.

A swimming pool area that is attractively lighted invites entertaining activity and casual conversation long after all swimming is concluded for the evening. Note the way light is reflected by white-barked trees.

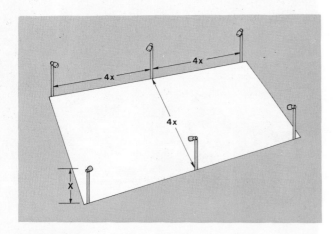

The four times mounting height ratio holds true for the distance across the area to be lighted as well as the lateral distance between poles. It applies regardless of the number of floodlights on each pole, or the level of illumination sought, or whether the light source is mercury.

For versatile activity lighting it is recommended that several outdoor weatherproof electrical outlets be installed so that the lighting can be changed for seasonal reasons, or when the area is to be used for another purpose. The outdoor outlets will provide desired flexibility and should be installed to handle from 300 to 500 watts, even though you might not regularly put that kind of load at the outlet. Such outlets can also be used for party lighting.

Generally, the PAR-type lamp (Parabolic Aluminized Reflector — see page 58) will be used for most outdoor floodlighting for it can withstand severe weather conditions and provides good general purpose lighting. The lamps can be attached to temporary telescoping portable poles if an area is only occasionally used for games. Activity lighting, because of its brilliance and mounting height, must be carefully planned and located so glare from the lights does not reach your neighbor's property. Separate lighting circuits are recommended for activity lighting so that they may be controlled apart from any other outdoor lighting on the property.

The following is a list of various recreational activities and the average recommended footcandles of illumination for each activity:

ACTIVITY	FOOTCANDLES
Archery	5
Badminton	10
Basketball	10
Croquet	5
Horseshoes	5
Shuffle Board	5
Tennis	10
Volleyball	10

Evening projects lightened

Some lighting on the outside of the home is almost entirely functional, and the only considerations that need be given are that the glare doesn't offend the neighbors and that the level of luminosity is sufficient for the work to be performed in the light.

Normally, this calls for floodlights to bathe an entire area in sufficient light, with little or no consideration given to attractiveness. It may be that such a light is convenient over the garage door, in a rear area used for working on projects after dark, or in the area leading to the garbage cans.

In some instances, dimmer switches in the outdoor lighting circuitry allow for the creation of high levels of illumination for utilitarian purposes, while also allowing the homeowner to reduce the light to a more relaxing level when he so chooses.

Light is security, too

Activity lighting and utility lighting can be used for security lighting. It is possible to wire the electric circuits to a panel located in the master bedroom, for example, so that the flick of a single switch illumes your entire property. Interior low voltage switching circuits are particularly adaptable to main panel control and can be installed in most homes.

Another approach to security lighting is to utilize an automatic timer switch or light sensitive switch that will turn on selected lights at a predetermined time or at dusk. Or these switches may control the level of illumination of the lighting so that a higher intensity is available during the early evening hours, and lower intensity lighting illumes the grounds until dawn.

In any event, light discourages trespassers, and the use of your outdoor lighting as security lighting is an additional benefit.

Actively used areas such as patios and lanais benefit from soft lighting for barbecues and entertaining.

An outdoor barbecue is more attractive and more useful with illumination at the working level.

Swimming Pool Lighting

Aesthetic appeal and safety at the pool

Beauty of illuminated landscaping is reflected from the darkened pool surface. Landscape Illuminator: John Watson.

A swimming pool offers almost as much pleasure as an area to view and as a background for entertaining as it does in the swimming it provides. With wide decks, comfortable pool furniture, and surrounding landscaping, a swimming pool is usually the dominant attraction on any property. This is particularly true at night with tastefully arranged outdoor lighting.

A pool has some of its greatest appeal after dark, as a background for patio entertaining or for a swimming party. Nor should the view of the pool from inside the home be forgotten—with the underwater lights off, the surface of the pool reflects the lighted landscaping surrounding the pool. Lighting can be planned to enhance the reflections viewable in the pool.

A first concern in lighting a swimming pool is the safety and level of illumination within the pool—the underwater lighting. In most average-sized pools, there is a light at the deep end of the pool several feet below the diving board. It is best if the pool has been located with the deep end nearest the house so that the glare from the underwater light occasioned by waves and splashing is directed away from the house. If your pool already has the underwater light located so that glare is directed toward the house, it is recommended that a dimmer be installed in the lighting circuit. In fact, John Watson, landscape illuminator in Dallas, believes that a dimmer should be installed with the pool lighting. It is his contention that a dim glow of light is all that is necessary to identify the edge of the pool to provide a soft background for parties, cocktail hours, and late evening swimming. Use full brilliance when children are swimming.

For relaxation, turn off the pool lights, and even the pool pump, so that the mirror surface of the pool can quietly reflect the surrounding landscape lighting.

In installing pool lights, make certain that the electrical codes are met. Some areas allow only low-voltage (12-volt) systems, while others allow for 120 volt systems if satisfactory grounding is provided.

Most outdoor pools provide for wet niche lighting (page 27) with sufficient cord to allow the unit to be brought out of the water for lamp replacement.

Interior and exterior lighting blend to provide safe level of illumination at the pool deck. Good lighting in the pool not only contributes to safety but also is attractive when viewed from inside the house.

For determining the wattage required for lighting the pool, multiply the pool area (square feet) by .75 and divide by the numbers of lamps to be used. Ordinarily, 300 or 500-watt lamps will be satisfactory

Various features should be considered when purchasing underwater lamps and fixtures for a swimming pool.

• Attractiveness of the visible portion of the lighting fixture. Many are finished in polished chrome and conceal the mechanics of construction around the niche.

• Design should be watertight and tested for casting porosity and leakage.

• Material of the fixture should be rust-resistant over a long life. Many are of cast bronze and stainless steel. Fasteners for the fixture are usually stainless steel or silicon bronze.

• Low maintenance is a factor, and the use of PAR reflector sealed beam lamps eliminates the need for cleaning reflectors.

• See that lamps efficiently spread the light where it is needed.

• Safety can be assured by checking with the local electrical inspector as to the grounding of a 120-volt system or the proper equipment for a low voltage (12-volt) lighting system.

Areas surrounding the pool can be accented with light to add interest and to increase illumination.

In addition to giving warmth, glowing charcoal in an expanded metal basket casts light on nearby plants.

In addition, consideration can be given to various swimming pool alarm systems for additional safety and security at the pool.

For the lighting of the over-all area surrounding the pool, a variety of approaches may be considered. Again, the contemplated use of the area is the place to start. Some landscape illuminators believe that underwater pool lighting can be sufficient for creating a glow of light at the pool deck to provide a relaxing atmosphere and one that allows safe passage at poolside.

Any overhead lighting used near the pool must be located so that it does not reflect from the surface of the pool to cause irritating glare in areas where guests are likely to be. Uplighting along the pool fence can furnish satisfactory levels of illumination, as can lights placed behind the fence and diffused through plastic panels located at spaced intervals along the fence.

For convenience in adding party lighting in the pool area, it is a good idea to consider installing a number of weatherproof electrical outlets well away from the pool perimeter and possible splashing. Low voltage lighting is well adapted to poolside lighting, and the transformer should be well grounded and protected.

The underwater lighting installed in this swimming pool not only provides for safety during swimming but also offers a luminescent area of major interest in the nighttime landscape plan.

INSTALLATION AID

For installing electrical power to the underwater lighting system, the local electrical codes for swimming pool lighting must be met, and a local electrical inspector must approve the installation.

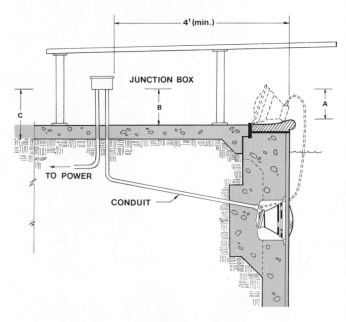

The diagram above illustrates the location of a junction box beneath a diving board. The local electrical code should be checked before installation to assure compliance. The junction box should be located a minimum of 4 feet from the perimeter of the pool. Although the diagram shows the junction box under a diving board, it could be located against a wall or fence as long as the 4-foot minimum is maintained. The junction box must not be located in a walkway unless it is protected, as by the diving board or other structure.

The junction box should be located 8 inches above the maximum pool water level (A), or the pool deck (B), or ground level (C), whichever provides the greatest elevation.

The diagram also shows the fixture removed so that the bulb may be replaced. Make certain that the light circuit is switched off during bulb change. Also, the cord in the niche at the fixture should be in good condition and not have any splices along its length. Most bulbs in swimming pool fixtures will last from 1000 to 2000 hours, so the wear on the cord from bulb replacement will not be too great if it is handled with ordinary care. When the fixture is replaced in the niche, the cord should be coiled carefully about the rear portion of the fixture. The fixture is then secured firmly in the niche.

Plastic panels reveal silhouette patterns as a background for amply lighted pool deck.

Lighting from overhead illumes the fence and nearby area. This interesting lighting treatment silhouettes the tree as a dominant feature. Landscape Illuminator: John Watson.

LANDSCAPE ILLUMINATION

Discoveries after dark

Darkness is but a curtain that hides your landscaping— a curtain that can be removed with the flick of a lighting switch to reveal the phenomenon of the night garden. This garden bears little relationship to the one that you see during the day, yet the beauty is distinctive— even enchanting. A familiar tree or shrub, for example, exudes a new personality, a new dimension, when captured in the glow of night lighting. Discoveries in the night landscape reach to the limits of your imagination. Creativity with lighting can be as challenging as painting, photography, or sculpturing. Darkness is a raw material—a black canvas—to be plied with light to reveal only what you want to see, in shapes and forms that may well surprise you.

Lighting for artistic effect is not new. In fact, electric lighting on the stage first occurred in Paris in 1849 —long before Edison's work on the filament electric light bulb. But, to a large extent, landscape illumination has been a neglected field until recently. One of the leading landscape illuminators, John Watson of Dallas, wrote the first thesis on garden lighting in the early 1940's after returning from Europe, where he had been amazed that the famous gardens of the continent were viewable only during the daylight hours. He based his career on the single premise that lighting can enhance the beauty of landscaping. Some of John Watson's works are illustrated on these pages to show the transformations possible in the garden at night by the addition of lighting.

Acceptance and use of residential night lighting has gained impetus with the advent of low voltage (12 volts) lighting, which is discussed in greater detail on pages 74-77. Basically, low voltage lighting offers the advantages of soft lighting effects and safety. Low voltage lighting systems are virtually free of hazardous electric shocks when they are properly installed. But most lighting experts agree that to properly light a large property, both standard voltage (120 volts) systems and low voltage systems should be used.

Landscape illumination, in general, offers the advantage of having two landscapes to enjoy. The sun-bathed garden looks much different than the same garden

selectively lighted at night. The sun gives every detail equal attention; night lighting can be selective of only those areas of the most interest. In fact, lighting often can create areas of interest that are non-existent during the day. For example, a tree or shrub near a fence may merely blend with the surroundings in daylight, but at night an interesting silhouette or leaf pattern is revealed.

There may be areas of the garden that are not completed or are in need of replanting—they are invisible at night simply by not being lighted. The new garden, when plantings are small, often is difficult to light in an interesting manner. A few larger shrubs or trees will often help create light and shadow patterns that add interest to the new garden.

A FEW TIPS

The measure of effective landscape illumination design is people—men, women, and children in pursuit of ways to satisfy their varied interests out of doors.

- People in motion outdoors require more space than they do indoors. For example, two people can walk side-by-side on a four-foot garden path, but a five-foot path gives them freedom to stroll and raise their eyes from the path. Illumination at night should also permit relaxed strolling along the path.
- Lighting should be planned with the intended uses of the landscaped area in mind. Consider whether outdoor entertaining is an important use, whether it is an area for children's activities, or whether the area to be lighted is mainly for viewing from inside the home.
- Lighting should also be planned from an aesthetic point of view to enhance nature and to blend with the lighting in the home. Lighting fixtures are concealed from view as much as possible, or are the kind that fit well with the landscaping during the day.
- Many lighting schemes are possible in most landscaped areas. Only experimentation will help you find those that are most pleasing. As one landscape illuminator put it: "Be prepared to spend many evenings walking on snails before the right effect is achieved."

Uplighting the tree and container planting provides attractive view through the window glass panels.

Landscape lighting seems to make the room more expansive. Landscape Illuminator: John Watson.

ON THE INSIDE LOOKING OUT

The extensive use of glass in modern homes presents large black expanses of glass at night, which, generally, must be concealed with draperies. The glass also reflects the lighted interior of the room, thereby repeating the decor in an undesirable fashion. Landscape lighting offers a pleasing alternative by providing a lighted scene that can be viewed from inside the house — a scene that actually seems to enlarge the spatial feeling within the room.

For avoiding reflective glare in glass at night, it is recommended that the levels of light be made variable. By increasing the level of light in the garden, for example, and reducing the level of light in the room, most of the reflective glare is eliminated. Varying light levels are most easily achieved through the use of dimmer units in the lighting circuits. Some dimmer units provide for only two levels of illumination, while other units allow for a complete range of illumination levels.

Reaction to outdoor lighting depends to a large degree upon brightness level. Subdued light is generally relaxing, but the level might have to be intensified if the lighting is to be viewed from a lighted room or patio. Merely floodlighting the area outside a window usually will not create any interesting effects, for such lighting is flat and offers few contrasts. A single object or plant spotlighted in the garden gives an unreal effect — a patch of light floating in a pool of blackness.

The photograph at the top right is a good example of landscape illumination providing a "picture" for a book-lined den. The foliage of the tree is lighted from beneath, and enough fill lighting is provided to complete the composition of the "picture" and to present interesting shadows along the fence. Note the different levels of illumination indoors and out.

At the lower right, a simply lighted garden gives a feeling of spaciousness in the room and adds to the perspective of the view. Four lights are used in the garden to offer a pleasant view that would otherwise be only black glass, or more confined with the bamboo shade lowered.

In composing a lighted landscape for viewing through a window or glass sliding-doors, it is good to keep in mind the basic elements of a lighting composition: namely, dominant lighting, secondary lighting, and fill lighting. For example, in the photograph at the upper left, the tree is dominantly uplighted, while the container planting to the left is of secondary interest, and there is sufficient lighting on the patio area to serve as fill lighting to prevent the feeling that the tree and planting rise out of a pool of darkness. Such lighting is somewhat akin to stage lighting when it is meant primarily for viewing only; however, when you walk into a lighted garden other aspects of lighting should be considered so that you are not annoyed by glare from unconcealed sources of light, and so that the level of illumination is such that safe passage is possible.

IN THE MELLOW MOONLIGHT

Quiet evenings and moonlight are familiar to all, and moonlight in the garden creates a particularly relaxing atmosphere. To achieve a moonlight effect with lighting is a challenge, but the result is well worth the effort.

Normally, a moonlight effect is created by lights supported among the upper branches of large trees so that the light filters down through the branches and foliage to cast interesting shadow patterns on the ground. There is a natural appeal in such lighting, and the over-all effect is soft and diffused. But the moonlight effect from downlighting is usually not enough to make a complete lighting scene, and therefore it is usually advisable to add additional lighting that accentuates a tree trunk or produces a modeling effect by lighting a shrub or planting from two different directions.

Note in the photograph at the lower left that the over-all effect is that of moonlight, but that additional

Orange geraniums in window box are highlighted with tube-type fixture. Landscape Architect: Kathryn Stedman.

Installation of a few lights in the garden removes the bleakness of dark glass areas and gives an added dimension to the room. A good level of illumination is maintained within the room.

The uniform, somewhat flat lighting of daylight can be observed in this patio view. See contrast below.

The same scene at night becomes more dramatic with landscape illumination. Landscape Illuminator: John Watson.

lighting has been added to accent the foliage near the windows, and there is sufficient light to eliminate black patches along the ground. The blend of indoor and outdoor lighting is at a comfortable, relaxing level, conducive to conversation and quiet enjoyment of the room and view.

LARGE AREAS MADE MORE INTIMATE

Large gardens or large areas need not present big lighting problems. The selectivity of night lighting can be advantageous. Even though the daylight view of an area is panoramic, certain features that are lost in the daylight view can be singled out and emphasized at night to form an interesting, intimate composition. In the daylight view to the right, a pleasant vista is presented with little or no emphasis on singular objects or plantings. A house is seen on the other side of the brick wall, which tends to show the limits of the property, and the general effect is that of flatness without perspective.

With landscape lighting, the photograph on the lower right reveals a lighted fountain and plantings backgrounded by light washing along the brick wall to give a feeling of depth. A tree is lighted to the right, and with light grazing the brick wall other trees are seen in silhouette. The house beyond the brick wall is unseen at night, and the filagree of the wrought iron fencing forms an interesting part of the background. Note that the illumination level is high enough along the ground to avoid isolation of the lighted areas.

Many landscape illuminators can determine a suitable night lighting scheme by viewing a garden during the daylight hours, but, for the person without a background of experience in landscape illumination, it is better to take an extension cord equipped with a hooded 100-watt bulb into the garden and place the light in various locations for assistance in visualizing the effect of night lighting before proceeding with the actual lighting installation.

In considering the installation of lights in large areas, plan on having a number of weatherproof electrical outlets installed at various locations in the area to be lighted. It is dangerous to run long extension cords from a house electrical outlet, and a voltage drop would result, thereby decreasing the efficiency of the lighting system. Extension cords six feet in length can be tolerated.

If you are contemplating a low voltage lighting system, the transformer should be located near the lighting system and the 120-volt circuit should be run underground to the transformer in accordance with the local electrical code. A transformer should not be powered by an extension cord over six feet in length.

A large garden area can seem to present a problem to effectively illuminate, but look for features that can be emphasized by night lighting. The photograph below shows how that was done in this area.

Compare this night scene with the daytime photograph above. The fountain and the filagree of the fence stand out dramatically, blend well with the lighted wall. A large area has been made more intimate.

Lighting a Small Garden

Only 12 x 29 feet

This small garden area is the same as the one photographed for the cover. Interesting lighting of structure has been blended with the lighting of the plantings. Light from the soffit facilitates viewing from the interior.

Many homes and ground-floor apartments have small outdoor areas that can be beautified by the addition of a garden. Or, perhaps, an atrium or small courtyard could benefit from a variety of plantings. In each instance, the area is generally in full view from one or more rooms of the house. Such areas are excellent candidates for night lighting, for the attractiveness of these areas enhances the adjacent rooms.

The design and lighting of small garden areas are a challenge to your ingenuity. One example of meeting this challenge is shown in the photograph on the left, which, incidentally, is also the photograph used on the cover of this book. A small area, only 12 by 29 feet, was lighted to create the illusion of spaciousness even though a complexity of access from three sides added to the problem—a problem that is common to many patio and dooryard gardens.

As the garden is to be viewed from indoors as well as for walk-through viewing, the lighting was made adjustable for the two viewing situations. The lighting equipment selected is in keeping with the size and scale of the garden. Some circuits are standard 120-volts, others are 12-volts.

In creating this lighted garden, the landscaping was planned first. Then a preliminary lighting plan was added. But for actual installation, the wiring for the lighting went in first, followed by putting in the plantings. The actual lighting fixtures went in last.

LIGHTING EQUIPMENT

The lamps on the roof overhang are 12-volt, 25-watt, PAR 36 floods, a good choice for uniform illumination without spill of light on the window glass. Small low-voltage units accent low plantings from hidden locations in trees. Another 12-volt lamp, semi-concealed in a small clump of ground cover, casts a sharp graceful shadow of a yucca plant on the fence. A Mugho pine is lighted by two unconcealed 12-volt, 25-watt, PAR 36 spots, using their beam control to avoid discomforting brightness in a visually critical location. Small low-voltage downlights on the fence add a decorative pattern of highlights and shadows.

Standard-voltage 150-watt floods at ground level also light the fence. So do blue fluorescents that create a background for tree silhouettes. Other lighting effects from standard-voltage lamps are: modeling and high-lighting on hemlock trees with 50 and 100-watt blue-white and 100-watt mercury lamps; moonlight effects with shadows and highlights on ground covers and paths created by 75 and 150-watt blue-white reflector lamps tree-mounted, or pole-mounted in small trees; uplighting from a ground-recessed waterproof incandescent lamp housing at the foot of the birch tree.

Downlighting grazes the slatted wooden fencing to present a sharp contrast of light and shadow in vertical rows.

The planting has been lighted from the front so that enlarged shadows are projected onto the fencing behind it.

Fine details of foliage stand out distinctly in silhouette against the lighted background of fencing.

Trees in the Night

Creating grandeur with light

A grove of trees lighted to provide interesting over-all illumination throughout the entire grove with a lighting level that permits safe strolling. Landscape Illuminator: John Watson.

If trees are part of your landscaping, you are fortunate, indeed. There is drama in trees. They cannot be ignored during the day, and should not be forgotten at night. Seek them out at night with light and they will reveal shadow patterns, textures, and foliage splendor not even imagined during the day.

Many descriptive terms have been applied to trees — graceful, stately, gnarled, ancient, wistful, stark, exotic, weathered, gargantuan, delicate, picturesque. With night lighting trees can also become romantic, ethereal, shimmering, luminescent, shadowy, and silhouetted.

A lighted maze of branches and foliage creates interesting shadow patterns on the ground below. Grazing bark with light accents unusual textures and reliefs. Light reveals the seasonal changes — the blossoms in spring, the ripe fruit of summer, and the panorama of autumn leaves. Even the stark branches of trees in the winter can create interesting silhouettes and shadows in a lighted landscape. The movement of trees in a summer breeze or a winter wind can be captured in an illuminated landscape — movement that would otherwise be lost in the darkness.

A tree can also serve as an important structure in lighting a landscape. Lights can be supported on the higher branches to provide effective downlighting. Such downlighting creates shadows and contrasting light patterns in a way that resembles the effect created by moonlight. It also provides sufficient illumination for a garden path, or for relaxed conversation on a patio or terrace. By using higher wattage lamps in the trees, an activity area below can be lighted for a game of croquet or shuffleboard.

Occasional uplighting in a tree helps to provide accent areas of light and makes the over-all landscape illumination more interesting. Viewed from a distance, the combination of uplighting and downlighting in trees can give an ethereal effect, as shown in the photograph to the left.

Trees are versatile performers in any lighted landscape and are an asset on almost any property where illumination is being considered. It should be mentioned that with trees, as with other objects to be illuminated, the total effect of all the lighting should be considered so that an interesting lighting composition is produced and that unpleasant glare from the light sources is concealed.

Here are several examples of trees that you can light, with suggestions on how to light them.

Acacia. The graceful, weeping *Acacia pendula* is an excellent tree to silhouette against a tall structure or skyline. Uplighting through its foliage reveals its interesting shape. The soft, silvery *Acacia baileyana* is almost self-illuminating. Floodlighting from a nearby

The design of this ornate lantern fixture as well as its light creates a unified scene with the group of trees.

Walnut tree with branches backlighted from below. Trunk is silhouetted against wooden fence.

Willow trees, with their lacy leaf structure, are easy to light for interesting effect. Landscape Illuminator: John Watson.

structure or tree will enhance its nebulous, cloudy form.

Birch. The birch tree has small leaves, open and flowing branches, and white bark which reflect almost any light. Even moonlight or lights from the house will dot the leaves with silver and accentuate the branches. Try a subdued light under birch trees, or a slightly stronger light hidden behind nearby full shrubs to accent their interest.

Brazilian pepper. This spreading tree has soft, feathery foliage that cascades from irregular and gnarled branches. Downlighting from the higher branches will spread the light over a greater part of the tree. Uplighting will allow the light to filter through the foliage in fern-like patterns.

Japanese maple. Small and delicate, this tree has a stepped or shingled appearance that is particularly suited to soft, diffused lighting from the base. A mature tree can be lighted by soft light placed at one side to illuminate it from tip to bottom.

Liquidambar. Lighting the dense foliage of this tree with a "grazing" light produces a pleasing effect. Lighting only the outer tips of the limbs with spotlights will create a chiseled effect of light and deep black.

Weeping willow. The unusual shape and continual activity of the branches make the willow tree a good subject for either uplighting or downlighting. A lighted willow reflects especially well on the surface of a darkened pool of water.

Multiple plantings of trees in groups makes an attractive lighted panorama. Landscape Illuminator: John Watson.

The delicate tracery of a Japanese maple is illuminated against the vertical lines of a battened wall.

A decorative lantern adds to the interest of the illuminated scene. *Landscape Illuminator: John Watson.*

Upper limbs of tree and the statue seem to be bathed in the same light. *Landscape Illuminator: John Watson.*

A tree in the entryway of this home has been dramatically silhouetted against a well lighted wall.

Low voltage lighting system uses six lamps to light entry garden, walkway. One lamp outside gate.

Lighting Plants, Too

For shadow, form, and beauty

Many plants reveal an exotic nature when lighted at night—a nature that is often not noticeable during the day. Lighting the underside of the ferns creates an almost luminescent effect against a dark background.

Major portions of most landscapes include plantings in a variety of arrangements. Most plantings, if not all, can be attractively illuminated for late evening viewing.

Lighting the landscape, for all practical purposes, provides two landscapes to enjoy. An array of plantings bathed in sunlight has a much different appearance than plantings selectively lighted at night, and in many ways the plantings are more dramatic at night.

There are five basic effects that can be achieved in lighting a planting.
• Floodlighting reveals the planting in much the same way as it is revealed during the day, except that shadows from the planting are controlled by the positioning of the floodlight.
• Spotlighting is selective floodlighting and can dramatize a single plant or a portion of it.
• Backlighting from ground level creates an interesting effect because it seldom occurs in nature. It is best on translucent leaves.
• Silhouetting shows shape and outline of a plant. A plant is seen in silhouette against a lighted background, such as a wall or fence.
• Shadows are a striking by-product of light. They can be elongated or heightened, depending upon the positioning of the light source.

Look at the plants in your garden and decide which kind of lighting suits them best. When the range of effects is understood, select the plants to be lighted as part of your over-all landscape illumination. Care should be taken in the use of floodlighting, for, basically, floodlighting produces a flat effect and may be of sufficient intensity to destroy the effects created by other lighting in the same area.

You can also experiment with reflected light, which has a softer quality than direct light. Try bouncing it off a light-colored wall or fence to create a diffused light source.

Lighting plantings near a walkway or driveway not only illumes the plantings but also provides sufficient light for safe passage on the walk or drive and helps to prevent damage to the plantings along the borders.

The following partial list may give you hints for types of plantings to light and ways to light them.

Acanthus. Its large sculptured leaves are well suited for silhouetting against a lighted background. Shining light through a plastic panel produces a soft light that creates a pleasing effect on the plant.

Azara. Soft, filtered light enhances the delicate, lace-like foliage of the plant. For delicate shadow patterns, place light directly at base of the plant. For wispy outline effects, place lights at a distance.

Bamboo. A small amount of light goes a long way

Lighted from the base, Mugho pine appears as a burst of light. Dense growth blocks glare even when viewed close-up.

Flower bed viewed in full color array when bathed in light. Contrast offered by vertical lines of fence and lighted panels.

Delicate nature of fern plantings revealed in both silhouette and reflectance against stark wall paneling.

During the day this quiet corner has a house in the background. The statuary and plantings do not attract immediate attention. Compare this with the lighted landscape in the photograph below.

At night the house in the background is obscured, and the brick wall provides an interesting surface on which to project the shadows of the small plantings. The statuary now is a focal point.

with bamboo. One effective treatment is the placing of a group of ground lights in the center of a clump, with each light turned in a slightly different direction than its neighbor.

Fern. To emphasize the fine, delicate foliage, light ferns from beneath. Small lights are best to avoid glare. The open nature of the plants does not hide a light source well.

Sedum. Taller-growing varieties, such as *Sedum praealtum*, grow in a tangled fashion that can be effectively lighted by a diffused light hidden among the plants or in the background.

Tree fern. When softly lighted from below, it can capture the feeling of an entire garden. Small shadows and sparkles weave over its foliage and filter onto nearby structures and plants.

It is always good to keep in mind that plantings grow and their growth may change or hinder lighting effects initially planned. Check occasionally to see if there is a need to relocate lights relative to your plantings.

Other plantings to consider for night lighting include these:

Agave	Gunnera
Aloe	Hydrangea
Azalea	Magnolia
Bougainvillea	Podocarpus
Camellia	Rhododendron

Plantings in containers or otherwise arranged outside a window can be lighted to provide an interesting night scene viewable from inside the house. Such lighting, when done properly, helps eliminate reflective glare on the window and tends to make the room seem more spacious. It takes relatively little light outside to reduce all reflections except those coming from a bright direct light. Experimentation with light levels inside and out will help you achieve a balance of light that virtually eliminates reflections on the windows.

In lighting plantings, as in other outdoor lighting, it pays to experiment before installing any permanent wiring or fixtures.

A flower bed in full color is captured at night with a row of mushroom-type fixtures spreading white light.

Several types of succulents in a planter have an almost eerie effect when lighted against a dark background.

Fountain & Pool Lighting

Combining water and light

Darkened pool offers an excellent surface for reflecting surrounding illumination of trees, plants, and nearby structures. The lighting composition is repeated in the pool and contributes to total beauty of the outdoor scene.

Fountains and garden pools can often be focal points in a landscaping scheme. Their beauty can be accentuated at night with illumination. Water, whether still or moving, is an excellent candidate for night lighting. It is hard to imagine a more relaxing combination in a garden than that of soft lighting and the sound of moving water at a fountain or pool.

Water, when still, offers an excellent reflecting surface for light. Or, with the light placed under the surface, water reveals the light much as it would be revealed through glass. It is the movement of water and the air bubbles produced thereby that give water a translucent quality—particularly movement caused by a fountain or a waterfall.

When lighting a pool, guard against both reflective glare and glare that may result from the placement of lighting under the surface. Overhead lighting shining down on the surface can produce glare and diminish the attractiveness of the garden pool. Special lily-pad lights that float on the surface, as shown on page 46, offer an easy way to light a pool, and the lily-pad conceals the source of light.

Lighting of fountains and waterfalls also requires special consideration in the placement of lights to avoid glare. Special lighting fixtures are available that permit the location of a light at the base of a fountain so that the light is directed up and into the fountain spray. If you like color lighting, this is an excellent place to try it, for the colored light is effective in the translucent fountain spray. If a light source is located behind a fountain, it can generally be seen, so it is advisable to shield the light source so that only reflective light is revealed through the fountain.

The fountain shown in the photograph at the upper right is lighted to produce deep shadows under the fountain ledges so that the streams of water are revealed in contrast to the shadow portions. Such lighting also reveals the texture of the brick supporting wall in an interesting manner. The end result is a pleasant fountain area that combines the visual effect of flowing water and the relaxing sound of falling water.

Small fish ponds also offer interesting lighting possibilities. The visual pleasure is increased in watching the aquatic life in the pool swim and dart in the underwater illumination. Landscape illuminators recommend an amber light for a pleasing effect.

To create the effect shown in the photograph on page 46, a low-wattage incandescent lamp in a watertight socket is secured at the bottom of the pool. A rock positioned directly above the lamp conceals the light source. If shielding had not been possible, a lily pad lighting fixture could have been used for light-

A lighting effect that captures the brilliance of the water against the shadows. Landscape Illuminator: John Watson.

Underwater light directly beneath acrylic plastic sheet casts rippling shadow patterns on water and walls.

Shielded, louvered floodlight shines down through leaves to illume pool area. Architect-owner: Henry Hill.

ing the pool. It is recommended that two to four watts of power be used for each square foot of water surface. The plantings at the pool are lighted by a low mushroom-type fixture. A ceramic figure is added for visual interest.

The photograph at the upper right also utilizes a decorative figure. The watching figure tends to direct attention toward the small waterfall to give the scene unity.

To add interest to the fountain shown in the photograph at the lower right, a 400-watt colorscope can be submerged in the center of the fountain to effect changes in color on the changing water pattern of the fountain. Such lighting effects are specialized, and care should be taken in the selection of the underwater lighting equipment. The dramatic effect, however, may well justify the additional effort.

Where a water spout falling into a pool creates a series of ever-widening ripple circles, an overhead light directed at an angle from a distance can create an intriguing effect with the ripples catching the light.

Low-voltage fixtures attached to floating plastic lily pads illuminate pool floor and surrounding walls.

Colorful plantings, frog, and fountain revealed at night by small mushroom-type lighting fixture.

Picturesque ripple reflections will be revealed on any background surface near the pool to provide additional movement in the lighted composition. Some movement in a lighted landscape is recommended by many landscape illuminators.

To add a fountain to your pool, numerous pumps and spray rings are available on the market to help you create a variety of fountain effects that will be attractive during the day and when lighted at night.

Some pools have small grottos, and the darkened interior of the grotto can be lighted to afford subdued reflecting light on the pool. Falling water at the grotto is illumed by light reflectance, or specially designed grotto lamps can be used.

Fountains and pools offer challenging possibilities for night lighting; experimentation will help you to determine the type of lighting effect that will be most pleasing in your landscape. It should be a separate project in itself, and you should check with your local electrical inspector before making the installation.

Water motion gains additional attention by location of statue that "watches" the pool. Landscape Illuminator: John Watson.

A lighted fountain and the sound of water splashing in the small pool make for an appealing landscape and a relaxing atmosphere in the late evening. Light is reflected by surface of walkway.

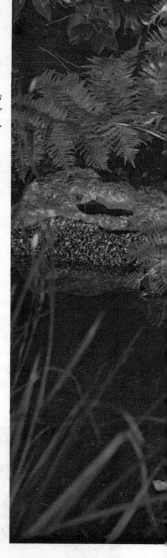

A variety of foliage from plantings and ferns reflect light from a low mounted fixture for reflection in a darkened pool.

LIGHTING TECHNIQUES

Tricks of the trade

Landscape illumination can be compared to the sleight of hand of a magician—you see only what he wants you to see. Diversionary motions are made so that you watch one part of his trick while an important action is accomplished outside your range of attention. The trick is fascinating even though you know it is a trick, and you are entertained by the magician's talent and dexterity.

Landscape lighting is much the same. Lighting may produce the effect of moonlight, but it is not moonlight. You light only those portions of the landscape that you want seen, and the effect diverts your attention from the source of illumination. A distinctive atmosphere is created. In short, the stage is prepared for evening viewing. Presto! A palm tree is brought out of the darkness as easily as a rabbit is brought from a hat.

Landscape illumination has a lexicon of its own that covers and defines many lighting effects. While terminology may vary in different parts of the country,

the lighting effects themselves are recognizable anywhere.

For convenience, names of the lighting effects are listed below. Many are readily definable from the name.

Uplighting	Shadow Lighting
Downlighting	Grazing Lighting
Floodlighting	Spotlighting
Texture Lighting	Modeling
Diffusing	Accent Lighting
Area Lighting	Silhouetting
Moonlight	Fill Lighting

Every outdoor lighting scene uses at least one of these effects. At first, it is difficult to know which effect should be used. Your choice depends largely on personal taste, the over-all effect desired, and the objects to be lighted. A study of the photographs in this book should help you recognize various lighting schemes that may be useful for your purposes. For example, the tree silhouetted against the lighted fence shown on page 29 may suggest an idea of interest to you.

Perhaps, the front entrance of your home could be enhanced by using one of the lighting arrangements shown in the chapter on "Need for Lighting."

Three basic points should be considered:

1. The object to be lighted
2. The source of light
3. The relationship of the lighted object to the over-all lighting composition

Almost any object can be lighted for a pleasing effect: tree, shrub, brick wall, statue, pool, or fence. A survey of your garden will reveal a variety of objects to choose from. Some will have more interest than others. Lighting a tree for reflection in a darkened pool is one example. The shadow patterns from a lighted planting shown on page 53 is another. A review of "How to Visualize Night Lighting" on page 8 will help you "see" other interesting candidates for night lighting. As a lighting composition consists of dominant lighting, secondary lighting, and fill lighting, you should note the relationship of the objects which are chosen for illumination.

The source of light is explored in greater detail in the following pages of this chapter. A basic principle, however, is: *Conceal the source of light.* Most lighting fixtures are designed to conceal the light source. Where the source cannot be concealed, choose a fixture that is attractive both at night and during the day.

Considerable experimentation is usually necessary to determine the best lighting effects for a particular outdoor lighting arrangement. Fill lighting is important in blending the dominant lighting elements into the scene to produce a pleasing composition of contrasting lights and shadows.

One or two nights in your garden trying your hand with lighting effects won't make you an expert, but the effects will likely be pleasing enough to encourage further effort.

On the following pages a variety of lighting effects are shown with accompanying sketches indicating the placement of the lights. Chances are that you will have one or more of the plantings shown in the following photographs, so in your experimentation you can attempt to duplicate the effect. It is not necessary to experiment with the entire lighting arrangement at one time. Rather, it is easier to get the "feel" of outdoor lighting by achieving one or two effects. Once the effects are achieved, you can consider how they blend into a total lighting composition. If a lot is quite small, a few lights may be sufficient to effectively illuminate a small group of plantings or a tree. For example, only a few lights were used in the scene shown on page 42.

Many landscape illuminators start with an over-all sketch of the areas to be lighted. Marks are then made on the sketch to show the location of the lights. From experience, illuminators know the effects that the selected placement of lights will produce, and, as a consequence, many landscape illuminators can plan night lighting during the day.

You will probably find that making a sketch is useful, too. It need not be elaborate, but it should indicate important plantings and any structures near the plantings. Existing structures may be useful in supporting some of the lighting equipment. Refer to the drawing of a home and property shown on page 9 for help in determining the areas of lighting to consider and the way in which they relate to the home and to each other.

As you experiment with various lighting effects, mark the appropriate light locations on the sketch, indicating the approximate distance between the lights and the objects lighted. When you have completed one area and marked it on the sketch, you will have a handy reference that will assist you in pricing and installing the lighting system. Installation is covered in the chapter entitled "Lighting Equipment," beginning on page 70.

Another advantage of making a sketch is that it helps you to see your property more objectively. There may be areas that you will want to change before proceeding with the installation of lighting. If you are going to use the services of a landscape illuminator, the sketch will aid him in understanding what you want to achieve with outdoor lighting and, perhaps, reduce the over-all costs.

EXPERIMENTING WITH LIGHT

Use a weatherproof extension cord with a clamp-on lamp. The clamp allows you to secure the lamp temporarily at a desired location so that you can step back and view the results of the lighting. Using two or more extension cords with lamps allows viewing of multiple lights at a selected location. A hood at the lamp helps conceal the bulb so that attention is directed to the lighting effect.

As should be expected, extension cord lighting will not give the same effect as fixtures designed for night lighting. But you will be able to see the difference between uplighting, downlighting, and other techniques and to determine how a particular shrub or tree looks best. By using bulbs of various wattages, different levels of illumination can be observed. Subtleties of lighting will begin to appear. The way in which different varieties of leaves reflect light and the shadow patterns they form can only be realized through experimentation. Hold the light near a brick wall or a fence to note the interesting relationship between light and texture of material.

Experimentation is also a good way to find out about the complexities of working with color lighting. Refer to page 59 for a discussion of color lighting.

CAUTION, PLEASE

Don't overload any household circuit. An average 15-amp circuit can safely handle only about 1,500 watts.

Do your experimenting when the area is dry—at least, as dry as it is possible to find it at night.

When working out-of-doors, never connect lamps into a hot circuit. Instead, install all bulbs and make all connections into a disconnected extension cord, then plug the extension cord into an outlet.

Use care when moving the bulb near fences or other structures so that the bulb does not break while the circuit is energized. The same care should be exercised near tree trunks and branches.

Any extension cords used should be in good condition. If more than one extension cord is attached to another it is advisable to wrap the connection with friction tape to prevent the cords from being pulled apart and to prevent water from entering at the connection.

In walking about the garden with an extension cord, do not put undue strain on the cord or allow it to rub against a rough surface or the sharp corner of a structure.

If you have a number of weatherproof electrical outlets, it is better to utilize the extension cord at the various outlets rather than connecting several extension cords together to reach the most distant areas.

Don't allow the cord to extend over or lie in any pools or fountains.

To assist you in outdoor lighting experimentation, the following photographs and drawings are presented along with descriptions of the lighting arrangements.

UPLIGHTING

A single recessed floodlight is directed up into the palm fronds. The glare of the light source is concealed both in the ground and behind the trunk. Some of the fronds are seen in silhouette while others seem to be glowing with illumination.

UPLIGHTING COMBINED WITH DOWNLIGHTING

A tree or grove of trees is particularly suited for combined uplighting and downlighting to illume the foliage and to cast shadow patterns along the ground. Note that the level of illumination is suitable for relaxed strolling.

The uplighting fixtures are positioned above normal eye level in order to prevent glare. The downlighting fixtures are secured high in the trees to flood a wide area with light and to cast shadows of the limbs and branches on the ground.

Weatherproof fixtures and bulbs should be used.

DOWNLIGHTING—WIDE SPREAD

Downlighting close to the ground is commonly used for walkways and bordering areas. Succulents, brick patterns, and small container plants add interest to the lighting scene, and the level of illumination is sufficient for safe walking.

The small mushroom-type fixture can be either standard voltage (120 volts), or low voltage (12 volts). The lighting should be checked from time to time to make certain that plant growth does not obscure its effect. Fixtures near a path are sometimes damaged by traffic.

DOWNLIGHTING—CONTROLLED BEAM

A pleasant corner where brick surfaces meet makes an ideal location for a variety of plants that can be illumed by a downlight reflected from one wall. Sufficient light is reflected to light the border of the drive and the decorative path.

PAR lamps with shields and narrow spots can be mounted on trees, poles, or nearby structures.

SILHOUETTE LIGHTING

One of the most well-known lighting effects and one of the easiest to produce. The source of light is located behind the object to be silhouetted so that the source is concealed. For most plantings the light is directed away from the planting and toward a wall or fence that is only a few feet behind the planting to be seen in silhouette.

LIGHTING FOR SHADOW EFFECT

A shadow appears behind a planting lighted from the front. With a wall or fence immediately behind the planting, the shadows are cast upon the wall or fence. By directing the light upward from the ground and close to the planting, the shadows appear large and dramatic. A wide beam light tends to spread the light more so that interesting shadows are produced on nearby fencing, and softer light falls on the planting. By positioning the light relative to the planting, you can determine the best shadow pattern for your planting.

A spike-mounted light fixture allows re-positioning to change shadow patterns.

GRAZING LIGHT

Texture and surface contour can be made interesting with light directed along and close to the surface of a wall, fence, or door. Such grazing light creates shadow and light patterns along the surface. Brick walls and stonework are particularly interesting when grazed with light. The light may be directed over the surface from a number of directions as long as the light is kept close to the plane of the surface.

MOONLIGHT

A moonlight effect is the closest to *natural* lighting. Soft light coming down through the trees produces interesting shadow patterns on the ground and often provides sufficient light for strolling. Fixtures that spread light down over a wide area are mounted high in the trees. The number of fixtures used will depend on the area to be lighted and the level of illumination desired at ground level. As foliage tends to break up the light and soften its effect, areas with trees are generally chosen for the moonlight effect.

LIGHTING AN ART OBJECT

Fences, walls, and entryways are often good locations for hanging mosaics and other art objects. Soft lighting from a low voltage system can provide flattering illumination for such works of art. Here the low voltage light source is mounted on the ground and directed upward at an angle so that shadows are produced to reveal the figures in detail. Such an art object can be more interesting when properly lighted at night than it is during the day.

ACCENT LIGHTING

Numerous types of fixtures can be used for accent lighting. Here the fixture is mounted in a roof overhang, and the light source is a 12-volt, 25-watt, PAR 36 lamp. The lighting effectively calls attention to an interesting detail in the garden and emphasizes beauty that might otherwise be lost with more general illumination. Statuary can also be dramatically revealed with accent lighting. PAR 46 lamps mounted in 16-inch-deep fixtures also make good accent lights.

LIGHTING FOR PERSPECTIVE

Achieving perspective in a landscape can be considered a major objective of night lighting. Good perspective can give the feeling of expansiveness and distance. Darkness tends to close in on a poorly lighted area to create a feeling of confinement. A view from a patio or terrace is more satisfying if the illusion of distance is produced with lighting. The same is true of a lighted landscape viewed through a window in the family room or living room.

The photograph to the left is a good example of the perspective that can be achieved with properly planned night lighting. John Watson of Dallas designed and installed the landscape illumination shown in the photograph. He considers it "one of the most rewarding gardens" that he has designed. "The lighting is designed to be majestic, and the cathedral-like columns of the trees enhance the religious aspect of the statue of St. Francis."

Note that the feeling of perspective is produced by lighting of the trees and path toward the statue.

DIFFUSING LIGHT

General illumination is the main aim of diffusing light and can be accomplished by using such equipment as lanterns, globes, wall brackets, and ceiling-mounts. In the photograph to the right, a single spotlight is mounted above a canvas panel to provide soft, diffused light at the picnic table. Almost any translucent material could be used for a panel on a frame of your own design. The panel not only reduces the glare from the spotlight, but also adds a decorative note to the picnic area.

LIGHTING FOLIAGE

Foliage and lighting can be combined with interesting and attractive results. The leafy sparkle and brightness in the photograph to the right is from a tree-mounted reflector lamp shining on the foliage. Some leaves offer more reflectance than others, and some leaves are translucent. Movement of the foliage in a breeze adds to the dramatic effect created by the lighting. Use white or blue-white light for the best results.

THROUGH THE GLASS—BRIGHTLY

Part of the secret of being able to view outside illumination through a window or sliding glass panel without the annoyance of reflective glare is to have a brighter level of light outside than inside. A dimmer on the interior lights facilitates changing the level of illumination on the inside. It is also possible to make provision for at least two levels of light outdoors.

The landscape illumination in the photograph to the left is the work of Kathryn Stedman, landscape architect. A tube-type fixture is used to highlight the orange geraniums in the window box outside the Stedman living room. The tree is bathed in soft light, and the fence beyond is lighted to complete the scene and to give perspective to the view through the window.

If there is an overhang outside the glass, 12-volt, 25-watt, PAR 36 lamps can be recessed to direct light onto a window box or a step. The eye is directed out to landscape illumination beyond, and the added light from the recessed lamps reduces the reflective glare on the window from the interior lighting. If a table or floor lamp is located near the window, its shade should be opaque.

AREA LIGHTING

Floodlights can sometimes effectively light a large area. Normally, the effect is somewhat uninteresting because of the even distribution of light from a floodlight. However, note the effect of floodlighting in the photograph at the left. The garden, designed by Chuck Ito, has much the same character, form, and color at night as it has by day. It becomes a continuation of the house itself, and the beauty of the garden replaces drawn draperies or cold black windows inside.

If the area to be lighted is visually interesting during the day, floodlighting will make it so at night, too. Here the shapes in the garden are attractive against the background of darkness.

Area lighting can also be accomplished with open flood units, glass-enclosed floods, and bare PAR floods. Usually such area lighting fixtures are mounted from 10 to 24 feet above the ground. Trees, poles, and structures may be used to support them.

Some area lighting is used for outdoor games and work around the yard. With a number of weatherproof electrical outlets and telescoping portable light poles, area lighting can be moved to various parts of the property, depending upon the need.

Area lighting also serves well as security lighting.

COLOR CAN BE A CHALLENGE OR A PANDORA'S BOX

Most outdoor lighting can be done with white light, but many people are likely to want to try color lighting. Taste in lighting is as individual as taste in clothing, interior decor, or garden arrangement. Innovations in lighting are occurring almost daily, and lighting is gaining acceptance as an art form. New color arrangements and light patterns, as exemplified in "light shows," reveal new ways to look at lighting —new ways to experience lighting. Consideration, therefore, of color in outdoor lighting is important. However, the complexities involved in using color lighting cannot be covered in this book, and while it is hoped that the reader will gain some understanding from the treatment of color that follows, he should realize that experimentation and further study are necessary if he is to obtain a working knowledge of the use of color lighting.

What is normally referred to as "color" is really "hue." Red, green, blue, and blue-green, for example, are hues. Within each hue is "value" or "brightness." Finally, there is "chroma," which is a reference to the purity of a color, or the extent it is free from gray.

Color lighting can produce surprising results for the uninitiated because of the combinations formed when colors overlap. When red and green lights are projected to overlap, the resulting color is yellow. When red, green, and blue lights overlap, the result is white light. Red light focused on a rose will accentuate the rose, but the green leaves will appear brown. Thus, lighting in the garden differs from working with paints on white canvas.

The primary colors in lighting are red, green, and blue, and from various proportions of these colors all other colors can be made to appear, as illustrated in the Maxwell Color Triangle shown below:

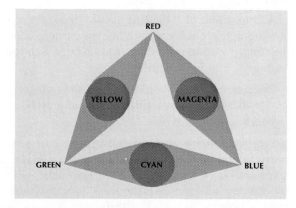

Maxwell color triangle illustrates color effects achieved by projection of the three primary colors.

Great care must be taken in working with colored lights in the garden, or the effects will be weird rather than pleasing.

In general, green foliage looks best in a green light, or in a blue-white light. Yellow light turns tree leaves brown, but it gives warmth to a house painted brown and creates a golden glow when directed on a white surface. White is the safest light to use on colorful surfaces. For example, a Santa Claus in a lawn decoration would still have a red suit in white light, but a yellow light would turn the suit orange; blue light would make it purple, and green light would turn it brown.

In color lighting, relativity plays a part. For example, if blue-green is surrounded with yellow the blue-green appears darker; it appears lighter when centered in a field of dark green. A blue background brings out green by contrast. This phenomenon is known as simultaneous contrast.

As color is primarily a sensation, there are many conscious and unconscious emotional overtones and reactions to color. In many respects, color lighting takes its discipline from stage lighting. A study of stage lighting reveals a correlation between color and emotion as shown in the following:

COLOR	EMOTION
Red	Danger
Orange	Warmth and excitement
Yellow	Contentment
Pale green	Kindness
Green	Macabre
Blue-green	Sinister
Blue	Quiet depth of feeling
Violet	Delicate emotion
Cerise	Deep affection
Lavender	Wistfulness

The above colors, when used in outdoor lighting, should be considered in conjunction with the color of the object or surface to be bathed in the lighting. If you use color when entertaining outdoors, you should consider the effect the color lighting will have on the complexions of your guests. Pink light, for example, is the most flattering; green light would produce a macabre effect and make most foods appear unappetizing.

Fountains and water sprays usually are pleasing when exposed to color lighting. For small ponds where the water is normally still, an amber light is suggested.

Interesting color lighting results are possible, but usually many hours of experimentation are necessary before an acceptable result is realized.

Dramatic form of tropical plants is accented by a weather-proof fluorescent fixture on the ground.

TIPS FROM THE EXPERTS

For quick reference, tips from landscape architects, landscape illuminators, and residential lighting specialists are set forth here to aid you in planning your own illuminated landscape.

Outdoor lighting, particularly garden lighting, seems more of a challenge than some people care to meet. In such event, it is often advisable to refer to professionals in the field of illumination. Ordinarily, a good place to start is with a landscape architect, or perhaps a local nursery will be able to recommend people who specialize in garden lighting.

To increase your own expertise, consider the following:

Purpose of garden lighting—All experts agree that this is the first determination to be made. How do you intend to use your garden in the evening? For relaxation, viewing, entertainment? Seasonally or year-around?

Levels of illumination—Two levels, at least, are recommended. It is desirable to have a lower level of illumination for relaxation and strolling in the garden, and a higher level for activities and for viewing the garden from within the house.

Perspective is important—Flat lighting without accent is usually monotonous. Perspective adds dimension and interest to an evening garden scene.

Do not light brightly at the property line—It tells everyone where your property ends and tends to eliminate perspective. It is better to highlight an object or planting a few feet from the property line, then locate softer lights at the line.

How does your garden grow?—Gardens are alive, so make sure your lighting arrangement is flexible enough to allow for changes caused by growing plants and shrubs.

Composition of a lighting scene—Basically, the following lighting is found in a lighted garden: dominant lighting, secondary lighting, rim or edge lighting (for statuary), and fill-in lighting.

Bounce lighting should be utilized—Often paths and walkways can be lighted effectively by bouncing light off a wall or fence.

Integrate home and garden—Light can create a unity of the interior and exterior of your home. The spaciousness of interior areas is seemingly increased by lighting adjacent exterior areas, and the home and garden become as one. Realization of indoor-outdoor living in the evening is made possible with light.

Grazing light effect—This can be seen by experimentally placing the light source close to a textured surface of a wall or fence and directing the light either upward or downward.

Attractive light structures can help unify—Light fixtures that are compatible with the architecture of the home add beauty during the day and are attractive at night.

Creativity and experimentation—It can be fun to experiment with lighting effects in the garden, and it calls for creativity, too. Numerous possibilities for lighting exist in every garden. Don't be discouraged with your initial attempts at outdoor lighting. An extension cord and lamp are recommended for experimentation. Place the lamp at various locations, then step back to view the resulting effects.

Some lamps can be adjusted from "flood" to "spot." The difference will be quickly noted by alternately floodlighting and spotlighting a plant or shrub. Two lamps will reveal the effectiveness of lighting an object or a planting from two directions at the same time.

Silhouetting—Direct the light away from the rear of a plant toward a wall or fence. The brightness of the light reveals the silhouette of the plant against the lighted fence or wall.

It helps to have a knowledge of plants—The effects that can be achieved with lighting are almost as varied as the plants in a garden. Some plants are more suitable for silhouetting than others. Some have leaves that reflect light more than others. Growth rates vary, and the lighting arrangement should allow for this.

Fountains and small pools—These can add to the attractiveness of a lighted garden. Moving water bathed in light is fascinating to the eye. A pool that is not lighted offers interesting reflections of surrounding lighting.

Safety and security—Any outdoor area can be more enjoyable at night if there is sufficient lighting to permit safe movement in the area. Light also discourages trespassers. Your grounds may be illuminated from dusk until dawn at a predetermined intensity through the use of dimming and timing circuits.

SAFE OUTDOOR LIGHTING

Condensed from numerous interviews and correspondence with landscape illuminators, landscape architects, electrical contractors, and manufacturers of lighting equipment, the following information and advice, if clearly understood and applied, should enable you to proceed safely with your own outdoor lighting system.

While there may be a number of reasons why residential outdoor lighting has not gained more acceptance with the homeowner, apprehension of electricity and electrical systems probably is one of the major reasons. It is one thing to plug in a new electrical appliance, but it seems to be an entirely different matter to plug in outdoor lighting for a garden or other outside area. Manufacturers of lighting equipment are well aware of this apprehension and do their utmost to produce safe lighting equipment and systems. Further, manufacturers rely on Underwriters Laboratory approval as well as detailed precautionary measures in their product literature.

It is well known that electricity is a useful servant, but it cannot be mistreated or mishandled. Wherever moisture is present, as it is with most outdoor lighting, care must be exercised in installing and maintaining lighting systems. Understanding the dangers and using extreme caution to avoid them is necessary. The purchase of approved equipment and reliance on people skilled in the handling of electrical equipment will further prevent hazardous electrical situations from arising.

Low voltage lighting systems have gone a long way in making outdoor lighting feasible as a do-it-yourself project in that hazardous shocks do not occur in properly installed 12-volt systems. The heart of the low voltage system is the transformer that converts 120-volt current to 12-volt current, and it is especially important that the transformer be of approved manufacture and that it have a grounded barrier to prevent the 120 volts from reaching the 12-volt wiring in the event of a short or other damage to the transformer windings.

Proper wiring and protective devices such as fuses or circuit breakers are a must with all electrical systems. Your local electrical inspector is well versed in electrical safety and should be consulted when you are considering the addition of any lighting system.

Worn and frayed wiring is always a potential danger. This is particularly true when moisture is likely to be present. Damaged lighting equipment should be repaired or replaced immediately. There is less potential hazard with low voltage equipment than with 120-volt equipment, but don't take chances with either.

In general, electricity need not be feared—just treated with respect. Knowledge goes a long way in dispelling fear, so when in doubt ask an expert.

Simplicity of lighting along the eaves and around the entry provides an inviting holiday or party effect. Lighting tree in abstract form offers contrast in line.

FUN WITH LIGHTING

Brighten holidays and parties

People smile when they're happy and in a festive mood. Set the stage for festivity with special lighting for holidays and entertaining. Outdoor lighting can be pleasing and relaxing throughout the year, but special occasions call for more decorative lighting.

The nature of the holiday will generally set the theme for the lighting. Christmas has been a time when most people are willing to try more flamboyant outdoor lighting, and more decorative lighting has traditionally been associated with Christmas. Centuries ago Spanish colonists in New Mexico lighted small bonfires of piñon wood along the paths to their churches to guide them to midnight Christmas mass. Later the New Mexicans began decorating their homes with *luminarias*—candles in paper sacks replacing the burning piñon wood—and this tradition has carried through to the present day.

Holidays and parties are events that often are remembered long after they are over. Extra effort is expended to make them pleasant. Lighting can be a part of that extra effort—an effort that can result in making an event even more memorable.

Decorative lighting does not necessarily mean overly-elaborate or lavish lighting. There is much charm and interest in simplicity. With too many lights, there is a danger that no one feature will stand out—there will be no focal point.

Holiday and party lighting, as with landscape lighting, often produces the best results when integrated with the interior lighting of the home. Such blending of lighting effects presents an inviting unity that extends a special greeting to passers-by and a welcome to your guests. An interesting holiday lighting scene in the front yard is keyed to holiday lighting within

the house so that visitors can react to the total holiday environment.

SELECT A CENTRAL THEME

To create unity, choose a central theme for the lighting and the objects to be lighted. A scene of Santa Claus and his reindeer will call for a different treatment of lighting than a scene of the Nativity. But, whatever the theme selected, remember that the principles of a lighting composition apply, and that the lighting will include dominant lighting, secondary lighting, and fill lighting (see page 8, "How to Visualize Night Lighting Effects").

Certain departures from your ordinary outdoor lighting can be taken when you are lighting for fun. The walkway to your home, for example, may be adequately lighted for safety and attractiveness, but not for festivity. Strings of Christmas lights may be used to light each side of the walkway, or they may be festooned along a series of upright poles to create an air of excitement on the evening of a holiday party.

In other words, holiday and party lighting challenge the imagination. Fun and lighting have long been close companions, from the earliest form of decorative outdoor lighting — fireworks — to the present-day extravaganzas of lighting at Las Vegas and at almost any centennial celebration.

The following pages show various approaches to holiday and party lighting as examples of some of the effects that have been achieved with decorative outdoor lighting.

HOLIDAY LIGHTING

A number of outdoor areas can be considered for holiday lighting. The major emphasis is ordinarily placed on decorative lighting on the front lawn, at the entryway, and on the front portion of the home. Such lighting is your Christmas greeting to the world and to visitors at your home—a preface to the holiday warmth to be found within the house.

Decorations chosen for the holiday scene need not be expensive. Many can be purchased, or you can fashion your own. But whatever the decorations chosen, they can be accented with light to be more appealing through the late evening hours. As light itself is decorative, care should be exercised in the selection of lights that are to be used in conjunction with your other outdoor decorations. Examples of over-decoration can be seen in many neighborhoods during the Christmas season.

A Christmas tree is usually part of every holiday decorating scheme. A lighted tree within the home is generally viewable from the outside, and an additional tree or trees can be set up on the outside. In the photograph on the right side of the page, a tree has been fashioned from a tall pole mounted on a porch roof. Colored roping spread from the top of the pole to the roof forms the outline of a Christmas tree. Strings of colored lights are intertwined with the roping.

How many Christmas tree lights?

It is difficult to over-decorate a Christmas tree. As for the number of lights to use, illumination specialists have suggested using the following formula:

Tree height in feet x tree width x 3.

On the average, the following table applies:

Height	Number of lights
4	35
5	56
6	77
8	102
10	210

A string of 20 outdoor Christmas lights using 9½-watt bulbs amounts to only 190 watts, about the same as used by a floor lamp. You can usually plug in three such strings to one house electrical circuit without overloading it. Many homes today have some 20-ampere

Simple cut-out figures add the holiday touch to this entry. Light directed toward the figures adds shadows and depth.

Miniature lights sparkle on hanging plants. Plants such as small-leafed ivy or asparagus fern can be used.

circuits (2,400 watts) and some 15-ampere circuits (1,800 watts)—either will serve for Christmas lighting. However, consider other electrical appliances that are connected to a house circuit before adding the load.

Bright little lights

The miniature lights shining on the hanging plant in the photograph at the lower left are becoming more and more popular as a part of holiday decorations. They are safe, and the bulbs give off so little heat that they do not damage foliage, paint, or other ornaments. Strings of these small lights may have twenty or more bulb sockets. Some are made for indoor use only, and others are weatherproof for either outdoor or indoor use.

Plain white bulbs come in two basic shapes: pointed cylinders imitating a candle flame, and slightly larger globes. Colored bulbs can be purchased for either of these shapes. There are also more ornate colored-light strings that have frosted bulbs or plastic reflectors.

All the bulbs must be firmly in place before the string will light. However, if a bulb burns out, the rest of the string will remain lighted. It is advisable to replace the burned-out bulb as soon as possible to prolong the life of the remaining bulbs.

Some of the small lights will twinkle—that is, they will blink on and off in random sequence or all together. If you like either blinking effect, ask specifically for the string that will produce the effect that you like.

The cord itself comes in green, white, or a neutral brown. The green almost disappears on an evergreen. The neutral shade is not much more noticeable. The white is intended for use with flocked Christmas trees and shows up too much elsewhere.

Placing bulbs just where you want them is much easier if wire garden ties are used. The ties are usually covered with green paper or plastic, and short lengths will keep the bulbs in the right place without the wire being too conspicuous.

When you arrange the lights, use lots of them and place them fairly close together. There is no glare and very little heat to worry about. A dense concentration of bulbs gives a striking effect. Many arrangements can be formed with these small lights, for the strings are lightweight and easy to handle.

Make certain that you purchase strings for outdoor use when decorating on the lawn or in the entryway. Use only heavily insulated extension cords, and keep the plugs protected from dampness. And, of course, be sure the electrical current is disconnected before you connect the string of lights to the extension cord. The small lights can brighten any Christmas in a safe and decorative way.

What better Christmas greeting than lighting that gives the effect of a towering pine over the entryway?

Christmas carolers in full view on holiday nights by using a concealed PAR lamp to light them from the front.

Angels and glitter on a paper background surrounded by a garland of pine brighten this lighted entryway.

SAFETY TIPS

With a large number of lights added to the electrical system during the holiday season, some may wonder whether or not the house wiring may become overloaded. In general, the extra electrical demand shouldn't overload house wiring that is adequate for the lights and appliances used in homes today. Christmas lighting usually amounts to less of an electrical load than turning on an electric oven, even if strings of lights have been run along the eaves and more than one tree has been lighted, or floodlights have been used to illuminate a display.

But you usually need to distribute this extra electrical load so that it is handled by more than one house circuit, because most of your electrical circuits probably already work at near capacity, particularly at night. Otherwise you may have an annoying blackout when someone turns on a lamp or the coffeemaker.

To determine the electrical circuit that various outlets are on, open one circuit breaker or unscrew one fuse at a time at night and note the sections of the house that are blacked out. The best outlets are weather-protected ones (such as on a patio or porch)

that are controlled by switches indoors. With these outlets, you won't have to plug in and disconnect a damp cord nightly on a live circuit.

Always exercise caution to prevent electrical shock when you connect outdoor lighting. Connect strings of lights to extension cords *before* plugging the extension cord into the outlet.

If you have to bring an extension cord in through a window to a dry indoor outlet, fit a wooden strip across the sill under the open window and bring the cord in through a notch cut in the strip. Then there is no chance of pinching the cord with the window frame.

If strings of lights are placed along the eaves of the house each year, consider installing small brass or plastic-covered cup hooks to hold them. The hooks may be more bother to install than insulated staples, but the hooks will be there ready for use each year and there is no chance of piercing the wiring, as a staple may do. If the strings of lights are subjected to strong winds, tape them to the cup hooks.

Use Underwriters' Laboratories-approved strings of lights that are marked for outdoor use. Check old strings for fraying, aging, and heat damage. Passage of

Soft lighting of a simply-designed holiday scene is accomplished by the use of a series of low voltage lights concealed in the shrubbery to cast shadow patterns along the front of the house.

time or overloading (and thus heating) the wires can harden and damage the plastic insulation of the wire. Such damaged strings should be discarded. To help keep water out of the light sockets, use the small rubber gaskets that come with outdoor sets and, where possible, arrange the cords so that the bulbs point down. Avoid wrapping wires around any downspout or other metal object that could abrade the insulation.

Whenever cords and light strings are connected together outdoors, keep the connections slightly above the rest of the cord so that water can drain away from the connection. If a connection is on the ground, place a brick or rock underneath it. Keep such connections dry by wrapping them with friction tape.

Any outdoor display that includes an electric motor should have a grounded three-wire cord with the ground wire connected to the motor frame. Make certain that the motor has a stable footing. Do not use extension cords of a length longer than that specified by the manufacturer. It is possible to burn out a motor if too long an extension cord is used.

Whenever several strings of lights or several floodlights are connected together, branch them out from a heavier cord that leads to the electrical outlet. Con-

necting one string to the outlet and the other strings in succession from it may overload the string nearest the outlet, which carries the current for all.

If a branch circuit is overloaded (blows fuses or trips breakers), remove some other electrical devices that are connected to it, such as floor lamps and kitchen appliances, and connect them to other circuits.

You can further safeguard holiday lighting by using small fused plugs available at hardware stores for about 25 cents each. To prevent overloading a wall outlet, plug one into the outlet and then connect the Christmas lighting to it. The small unit contains a 6-ampere (720-watt) fuse that will blow when too many strings of lights are connected to it. Even more important, the relatively weak fuse will blow if there is any kind of short-circuit in the strings. But even with these fused plugs, the load should be distributed over more than one house circuit. If several fused plugs are connected to outlets on a single circuit, they may not blow individually, but the house circuit may be overloaded and its fuse or breaker will go.

Safe lighting practices will not only keep the holiday season bright, but will help assure that it is an enjoyable one, also.

PARTY LIGHTING

Outdoor entertaining is becoming more and more popular, and with the use of lighting this kind of entertaining can easily be extended through the late evening hours. In one sense, the landscape illumination discussed in this book pertains to party lighting in that it forms an excellent environment for outdoor entertaining, both in establishing mood and giving guests a sense of well-being. However, as with holiday lighting, party lighting sometimes occasions a more festive approach than is taken in most landscape illumination.

Some people like to establish the feeling of a party atmosphere at the entryway or along the walkway to the entry. In the photograph at the left, two potted trees are decoratively lighted with strings of miniature lights to add a warm, welcoming note at the entryway. Another form of party lighting at the entry is shown in the photograph at the far right. In each case, the added lighting at the entry helps establish a party mood and heightens the expectations of the arriving guests.

However, the actual outdoor entertaining will usually take place on a patio, around a barbecue, at the swimming pool, or in a garden area. Whatever area you select, make the lighting say "partytime."

The availability of a number of weatherproof electrical outlets in the patio and garden areas will offer flexibility in making various party lighting arrangements. Existing landscape lighting can sometimes be changed to give a party effect by placing colored plastic caps over the existing light fixtures. Some low voltage lighting systems come in kit form with the color attachments forming part of the kit. When working with color, however, some experimentation is advised before the party to see if the colored light gives you the effect you want. See "Color Can be a Challenge" on page 59.

More party lighting suggestions

A colorful addition to party lighting can be made with rayon or translucent plastic panels. The panels in various colors can be secured to wooden frames made of 1 by 1-inch lumber, about 4 by 6 feet in size. The completed frame and panel is mounted upright in front of a fern planting or other planting having interesting foliage. By directing a spotlight onto the plant toward the panel a large silhouette of the planting can be seen on the reverse side of the panel. Any movement of the plant in a breeze will give the colorful effect of a dancing silhouette. A number of these silhouette panels around the party area will make a festive background.

Potted trees, pruned as globes and lighted with miniature lights, lead guests along entry path to a party.

For a colorful water fountain, an ordinary lawn sprinkler can be placed on a 2 by 2-foot sheet of ¼-inch colored translucent plastic mounted on a frame made from 2-by-4's. Place a weatherproof light under the frame so that the light is directed up toward the sprinkler. When the sprinkler is turned on, the spray of water will be caught in the colored light. It is best to use low voltage lighting for this impromptu fountain to reduce the hazards in the wet area.

The party lanterns shown in the photographs on this page can be fashioned easily from tin cans. Any size can is suitable. Fill each can with water to ¼ inch below the rim and place it in the freezer for about two days. Then cut a piece of heavy paper large enough to fit around the can, and draw a design on the paper. Fasten the pattern around the can with cloth tape or masking tape. Place the can on a folded towel. Punch holes in the can along the lines of the design as shown in the photograph below. A low voltage bulb attachment can be fastened to the bottom of the can so that the lantern can be used with a low voltage system, or a candle can be used.

Party lighting allows full use of your ingenuity to add a pleasing decorative note to your entertaining.

Ice frozen in an ordinary tin can facilitates punching of holes with a nail to make a patterned party lantern.

Decorative party lanterns fashioned from tin cans arranged to create party mood at the entryway.

Ground-hugging welded lamp has opening in its top to facilitate bulb changing. Top is galvanized and won't rust; bottom portion has rusted to a handsome burnished red.

LIGHTING EQUIPMENT

Fixture selection and installation

Many manufacturers are now able to furnish outdoor lighting equipment for almost any landscape illumination system. Some manufacturers work closely in the actual installation of lighting so that they are able to determine needs as they arise in the field and to improve fixture design. Ordinarily, however, the manufacturers of lighting equipment do not do the installation work.

Although there is considerable outdoor lighting throughout the country, only a small portion of it is residential lighting. For the homeowner, outdoor lighting is relatively new—at least, he probably hasn't seen many residential lighting installations. However, with the increasing acceptance of low voltage lighting, it is possible for the homeowner to approach outdoor lighting on a do-it-yourself basis. Though this book refers to both standard (120-volt) systems and low voltage

(12-volt) systems, emphasis is placed on low voltage systems in this chapter to assist in the do-it-yourself approach to outdoor lighting—particularly in the area of landscape illumination. This does not mean that standard voltage systems cannot be installed by the homeowner, but many people are reluctant to work with 120-volt wiring.

You probably will not light your entire property at one time but, rather, will want to approach it one step at a time. A review of the chapter entitled "Need for Lighting," on page 6, and the sketch on page 9 will help you select various areas in which to begin your outdoor lighting project.

Having decided to light a particular area, you should note the answers to the following questions in conjunction with a rough sketch of the area:

1. What is the size of the area in square feet?

2. What use will be made of the area?

3. Have weatherproof electrical outlets been installed? How many?

4. Approximately how many lights are needed for the area?

5. If you are planning on installing a low voltage system, will you need more than one transformer?

6. Are there enough structures and trees in the area for mounting overhead lights? (If not, you can consider telescopic poles that are portable.)

7. What amount of maintenance will be involved in the system? (See page 79.)

8. Do you intend to incorporate automatic timing devices and dimmers, or a master switch?

The following pages should help clarify the above eight points. Having answered these questions, you will be better informed when you discuss your proposed lighting system with a dealer of lighting equipment or a landscape illuminator. Chances are, in many parts of the country, you will be educating the dealer, but the end result will be a better lighting system for you.

In addition, a section about decorative lighting fixtures has been included in this chapter. It may give you ideas for making some of your own fixtures and, perhaps, make you aware that many objects can be turned into lighting fixtures with little effort.

Before proceeding with the actual installation of a lighting system, note that electrical codes and their interpretations vary throughout the country. Discuss your proposed installation with your local electrical inspector, and obtain his approval of the system. Most manufacturers base their instructions on the code.

Low Voltage Systems

Safe, decorative illumination

Low voltage lighting systems have gained in popularity because they are generally considered safer and easier to install than standard voltage systems. For this reason, many manufacturers of low voltage equipment have directed much of their effort toward the do-it-yourself market. In some respects, low voltage systems are not as expensive as standard voltage systems, but this depends upon the lighting system and the lighting effects to be achieved.

One reason for the introduction of low voltage lighting is that soft lighting can be obtained more efficiently with low voltage bulbs than with low wattage, 120-volt bulbs. Another reason is that the low voltage open wire systems can be installed without the need of conventional conduit, boxes, and other components that are required for 120-volt circuits. Installation costs are therefore lower, and the average low voltage installation can be a do-it-yourself project.

Six lamps dramatize small garden at end of car port. Light creates shadow pattern from magnolia and acanthus, right; silhouettes rocks, nandina, Japanese maple, center; emphasizes acanthus, fatsia, poplars lighted from below, left.

HOW TO INSTALL A LOW VOLTAGE SYSTEM

A low voltage transformer should be mounted near a 120-volt electrical outlet. Choose a transformer of about 100-watt capacity that has a grounded shield between the primary and secondary windings (the grounded shield is a recommended safety feature that prevents the 120 volts from reaching the 12-volt wiring). Most transformers have a six-foot length of cord for plugging into the 120-volt outlet (do not add an extension cord to this cord, for it may cause the transformer to fail). In an outdoor area, the outlet must be of weatherproof construction and installed in accordance with local electrical code requirements.

Two-wire No. 12 cord, not to exceed 100 feet, is attached to the low voltage side of the transformer. Larger wire sizes may be used.

Low voltage transformer mounted on fencing is connected to a weatherproof electrical outlet protected by the fence.

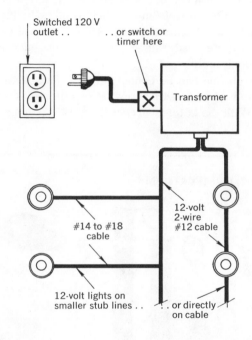

Low voltage light fixture is constructed so that it can easily be crimped into the wiring at the desired location.

Extend the low voltage wiring from the transformer into the garden or other area to be lighted. The wiring can be placed on the ground and need not be buried. An example of wiring from the transformer is shown on the above schematic diagram. Smaller stub lines can be spliced into the No. 12 wiring.

The low voltage fixtures are attached to the wiring at the desired locations. Normally, six fixtures can be located along the 100-foot length. Some fixtures are constructed so that they can be clipped directly to the wire, as shown in the center photograph on the right. Such fixtures can be relocated easily by merely unclipping them and attaching them again at another portion of the wiring. Other types of low voltage lighting fixtures must be spliced into the wiring system.

Low voltage fixture is attached to the wiring in a position to illuminate the steps. The fixture is weatherproof.

After the wiring system has been located in the selected outdoor area and the lighting fixtures placed to provide a planned lighting effect, it is time to consider whether or not the low voltage wiring should be concealed underground. If you plan to move the lighting system from time to time, it is better to leave the wires on the surface of the ground. However, burying them gets the wires out of the way where they will not be damaged or tripped over.

Wire may easily be put underground by inserting a spade into the turf at about a 45 degree angle to a depth of 6 to 8 inches for the length of the wire. Place the wire in the cut made by the spade and tamp the turf back to its initial position. The wiring will be concealed and the lawn will not be damaged.

Protection of low voltage wiring

In garden areas, you may want to protect the underground wiring by placing 1 by 3-inch scrap lumber over the wire as shown in the sketch at the right. The lumber will prevent the wire from being inadvertently severed by a spade or other digging tool. If any direct burial cable for a 120-volt system is in the garden, it can and should be protected in the same manner.

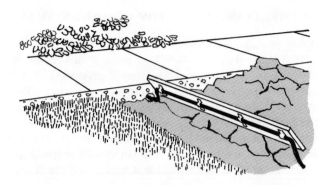

Low voltage wiring, placed 6 inches deep where possible, can also be run alongside walks, fences, planter-bed edgings, and structures to protect wires from damage from cultivating.

Stub lines (see page 73) can be used when installing a fixture on a fence or above an entryway. You do not need to run the stub line further to other lights, and it can be small wire, even No. 18 wire, which can be hidden quite easily along wood and masonry joints and along moldings.

A stub line can be connected to a main wire with soldered joints or with screw-on or crimp-on connectors. With the latter two, coat the finished connections

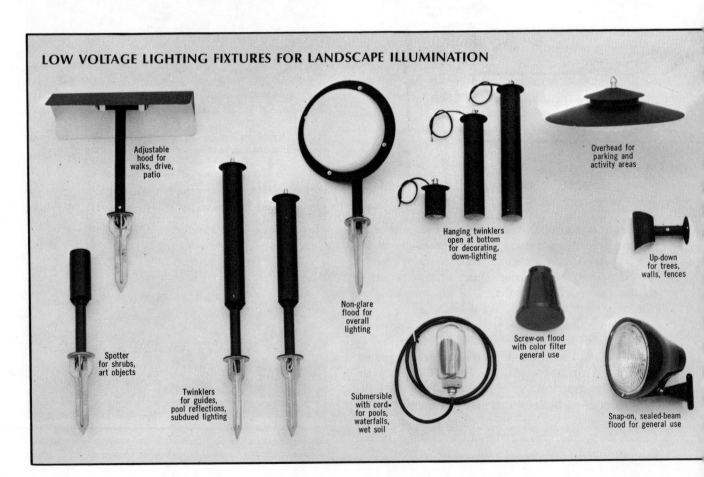

LOW VOLTAGE LIGHTING FIXTURES FOR LANDSCAPE ILLUMINATION

Adjustable hood for walks, drive, patio

Overhead for parking and activity areas

Hanging twinklers open at bottom for decorating, down-lighting

Up-down for trees, walls, fences

Non-glare flood for overall lighting

Spotter for shrubs, art objects

Twinklers for guides, pool reflections, subdued lighting

Submersible with cord for pools, waterfalls, wet soil

Screw-on flood with color filter general use

Snap-on, sealed-beam flood for general use

with any rubber seam compound—not for shock protection, but to prevent fertilizers and the like from corroding the connections.

OUTDOOR LIGHTING FIXTURES

A number of fixtures are shown in the photographs at the bottom of these pages. Some of the commonly used fixtures can be found there, but many other shapes and sizes are available on the market. In many installations, some of the fixtures will be concealed and some will be noticeable during the day. For this reason, a large number of fixtures are available in a shade of green that blends well with most landscapes. Other fixtures are meant to be entirely functional, and their shape is determined by their function. An example is the mushroom fixture that is often found along walkways or flower beds. The mushroom shaped shield conceals the light source and directs the light downward to the walkway or flower bed.

All outdoor fixtures should be of weatherproof construction and sturdy enough to withstand occasional blows that could result by chance from work being done in the garden or from children's activities. Most fixtures are made from metal or sturdy plastic.

Make your own fixtures

Making your own light fixtures from some wood, masonry, ceramic, or metal item on hand is simplified with one of the low voltage sockets shown in the sketch below. It can be attached with screws, bolts,

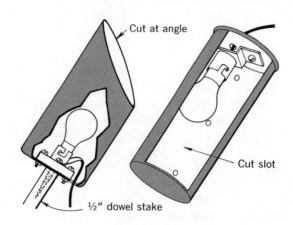

Cut at angle

Cut slot

½" dowel stake

solder, or epoxy glue, depending on the material of the fixture. The sketch shows lights made from ordinary aluminum cans.

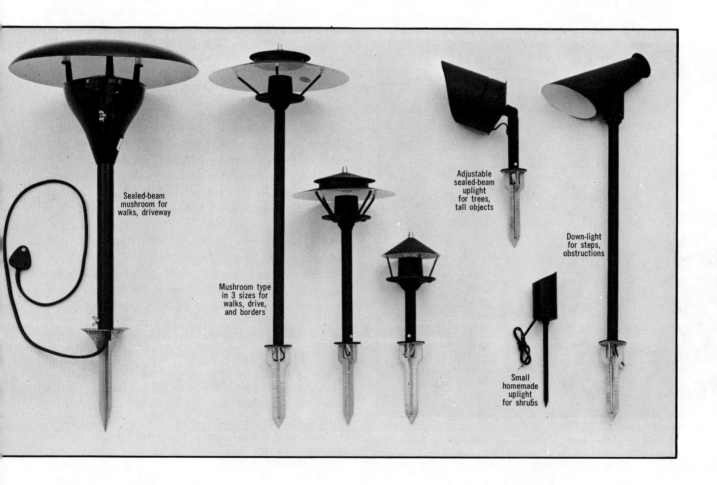

Sealed-beam mushroom for walks, driveway

Mushroom type in 3 sizes for walks, drive, and borders

Adjustable sealed-beam uplight for trees, tall objects

Down-light for steps, obstructions

Small homemade uplight for shrubs

OTHER TECHNICAL CONSIDERATIONS

Certain technical considerations should be made before purchasing or installing a low voltage lighting system if you are going to handle the entire project yourself. The following questions should be answered:

1. What is primary electrical supply voltage?

2. How many lamps are to be lighted?

3. What kind of transformers are needed to supply wattage to all the lamps?

4. What voltage loss or drop can be expected? (Wire size and length of wire are important here.)

The following information is presented to aid you in answering the above questions.

The primary electrical supply voltage available at your home can vary, depending upon the area that you live in, from 115 volts to slightly over 120 volts. For every 5-volt variation in primary voltage, there is about a ½-volt variation at the secondary voltage terminals of a low voltage transformer. An example of the effect of primary voltage variation on secondary voltage available at the transformer is as follows: At 115-volt primary voltage, a secondary voltage of 12.1 volts is produced at a particular load; at the same load and a primary voltage of 120 volts, the secondary voltage is 12.6 volts.

A variety of low voltage bulbs are available for producing different lighting effects—from sealed beams on down in size.

Bulb life and brightness

In low voltage systems, the voltage at the bulb has a great deal to do with bulb life and brightness. As the voltage is lowered the bulb life is extended, but there is a loss in brightness from the bulb. If, for example, 100 per cent bulb life can be assumed at 12 volts, the bulb life will increase to about 300 per cent when the bulb operates at 11 volts, but the brightness will drop from 100 to 75 per cent. One way of regulating and changing the voltage to the bulbs is by the addition of a dimmer switch. (The dimmer may be of the solid-state type, but of a type specifically designed for use in the primary of a transformer.)

By adding the total wattage of the bulbs to be lighted from a single transformer circuit, the size of the transformer can be determined. The load should be at least half of the rated load of the transformer. If the transformer is rated at 100 watts, the load should be over 50 watts, such as would be the case with six 10-watt bulbs.

Voltage drops also occur along the length of the wiring. The bulb farthest from the transformer experiences the largest voltage drop. For this reason, most manufacturers of low voltage lighting systems recommend that not more than 100 feet of wire be connected to any one transformer. The size of the wire also makes a difference in the amount of voltage drop. Number 10 wire, for example, will produce less voltage drop than Number 18.

National and local electrical codes

The National Electrical Code and most local and state codes have provisions that are applicable to the installation of outdoor wiring. Compliance with these provisions follows the same pattern as for any other new installation or rewiring within the house. Because local practices and requirements are not always uniform, specific code requirements have not been set out in this book.

As a general rule, however, most codes and ordinances covering fixed and portable equipment (lighting, appliances, tools), whether used indoors or outdoors, require that the equipment be electrically grounded. The usual method for accomplishing grounding of outdoor installations is to connect the exposed non-current-carrying metal parts of the equipment to the grounding conductor that is part of the branch circuit.

Any circuit installed in an existing dwelling for outdoor use should be a new circuit originating at the panel board rather than an extension of an existing circuit. In a new house, or in a house that is being rewired, the circuits for outdoor use should also be restricted to this purpose only.

LIGHTING SYSTEM MAINTENANCE

When you purchase lighting equipment, one factor to consider is the amount of maintenance the fixtures will require. Maintenance should also be one of your considerations in the original planning of an outdoor lighting system.

A leading landscape illuminator made the following remarks: "On the installations that I design, maintenance is considered almost equal to aesthetics. It is foolhardy to spend money and time on an intricate design of lighting that the owner has no intention of maintaining or where the maintenance costs would be overwhelming in later years. I suggest to my clients that they consider, in some cases, a more expensive investment in lighting that will mean, eventually, much lower maintenance costs."

One of the most common maintenance tasks is that of changing bulbs in outdoor lighting fixtures. The life of light bulbs will vary, depending upon wattage, type of construction, and operating voltage. Some bulbs will last only 400 hours, while more expensive gas discharge lamps may burn for 24,000 hours. A dealer or landscape illuminator can tell you the approximate hours of burning that can be expected from various bulbs. In choosing bulbs or lamps for high, hard-to-reach fixtures, select those with greater burning hours as long as they provide the desired level of illumination.

WHEN FIXTURES ARE MOVED. Permanency and stability of the lighting system installation is another consideration. Much will depend on the kind of system you want and the contemplated uses of the lighting. If you have small areas that you want to illume, and you want to be able to shift the lighting, for example on a seasonal basis, then spike-mounted fixtures that can be moved easily should be used. Many low voltage systems offer such flexibility, and some 120-volt systems can be as flexible if weatherproof outlets are provided in the various areas to be lighted.

However, part of the price paid for flexibility will be in the adjustment and readjustment necessary to produce the desired lighting effects. Quite often, even squirrels and birds can knock lights out of adjustment if they are not securely positioned. Valuable time can be required for readjustment of lights, and sometimes the need for adjustment comes just before an outdoor party when many other details are pressing for attention.

When spike-mounted fixtures are used, check them after a heavy rain, for some of them may fall as the spike loosens in the rain-soaked soil. Even small movement at the spike may change the lighting effect.

Children and their activities can occasion maintenance problems. If children's play areas are to be lighted, consider placing the lights high overhead.

WHEN WINTER COMES. Some landscape illuminators recommend that lighting equipment be taken inside during extended winter seasons, but much of the equipment manufactured today will serve well through extreme snow and rain conditions. However, before the winter or rainy season begins, it is advisable to check your lighting system to make certain that all connections and bulbs are properly secured and that any exposed wiring is well insulated. Transformers used in low voltage systems should be the all-weather type or should be protected from the weather in a sheltered location or with a weatherproof structure.

In areas exposed to salt air, consider lighting equipment constructed of plastic or aluminum alloys. However, it is a good idea to check with the dealer or manufacturer of lighting equipment, for many of the finishes provided are suitable for all climate zones.

Any lighting fixtures located overhead should be checked periodically to make sure they are securely fastened to the supporting structure. Changing bulbs before the winter begins will eliminate a climb in inclement weather.

INCREASING BULB LIFE. In maintaining low voltage systems, it is recommended that any burned-out bulbs be changed as soon as is practical. A burned-out bulb allows an increase in voltage at the other bulbs in the system, and as a consequence their burning life is shortened.

Another way to increase bulb life in a low voltage system is to install a dimmer. With a dimmer, the voltage to the system can be lowered to increase the life of the bulbs. Additionally, a dimmer in the system allows for the selection of a variety of illumination levels.

Attention should be given to the growth of plants and trees, for the increased spread of foliage may interfere with the lighting effect. In some instances, the planting can be trimmed back, but there is always the possibility that relocation of the light fixture may be necessary. Also, remove any leaves that accumulate on light fixtures. Heat from some lamps can start a fire.

In general, maintenance of outdoor lighting systems is not onerous, but it is necessary. And the exercise of preventive maintenance can reduce over-all maintenance costs and time required for making repairs.

Decorative Fixtures

Attractive both day and night

Most lighting fixtures manufactured today are of appealing design, for the manufacturers know that many fixtures are observable during the day even though the main purpose of the fixtures is to provide night lighting. Ordinary lighting fixtures are not meant to be major attractions in a landscape, but the fixtures shown on these two pages can be an attractive addition to your landscaping scheme as well as provide illumination at night.

Decorative fixtures can be used to add an accent to the garden, the patio, and other areas around the home. They are constructed of a variety of materials and can be wired for either 120 volts or 12 volts, depending upon the system you choose. If the decorative fixture is to serve a function such as lighting steps or an entryway, 120-volt bulbs will provide the most illumination.

Such fixtures are not usually found in stores selling electrical equipment but will probably be found at garden centers, art shops, and other specialty shops. In many instances, landscape architects and architects design decorative fixtures for a specific installation.

Often the structure of a decorative fixture adds a note of contrast to the foliage and plantings in a garden. Some decorative fixtures are really works of art that have been transformed into fixtures by the addition of a lamp socket and wiring.

Clean-lined, modern pottery fixture illuminates steps through pattern of holes. Design has somewhat whimsical feeling.

Light shines through circles and slits in a fixture that also serves as garden sculpture during daylight. Design: Al Dreyer.

Wood, colored glass fixture marks entry and steps, blends well with design of the house. Design: Al Dreyer.

Fire-glazed clay lamp placed over a standard fixture has not weathered, retains original appearance. Design: Ann Johnson.

Large suspended globe diffuses light over patio area to supplement light spilling out from inside the house.

PHOTOGRAPHERS

WILLIAM APLIN: pages 16 top and bottom, 60. ERNEST BRAUN: pages 4, 11 top left and bottom left, 17 right and bottom left, 23 top, 26 top, 37 bottom, 44, 54 top, 58 bottom, 73 bottom. CLYDE CHILDRESS: pages 30 top, 31 top, 38 bottom right, 39 bottom right, 41 top, 43 right, 52 top, 53 top, 57 top, 58 top, 72. GLENN M. CHRISTIANSEN: pages 68, 73 top and center. DESCANSO GARDENS: pages 40, 47 bottom, 49. RICHARD FISH: page 78 left. FRANK L. GAYNOR: page 25 bottom. GENERAL ELECTRIC COMPANY: cover, pages 7, 11 top and center, 15 bottom, 18, 27, 34, 35 top, center, and bottom, 37 top, 43 left, 46 bottom right, 51 top, 53 bottom, 55 bottom, 57 bottom, 63, 64 left, 66 right, 67. ART HUPY: page 45 bottom. ROY KRELL: page 79 top left. JACK MCDOWELL: pages 39 bottom left, 41 bottom, 55 top. DON NORMARK: pages 41 center, 71, 78 right, 79 bottom left. ROGER STURTEVANT: page 46 top. TENNESSEE VALLEY AUTHORITY: pages 17 top left, 19 bottom left and right, 23 bottom, 26 bottom, 31 bottom, 33 top and bottom, 42 top and bottom, 52 bottom. JOHN WATSON: pages 10, 14, 15 top, 19 top, 24, 29, 30 bottom, 32 top and bottom, 36, 38 top and bottom left, 39 top left and right, 45 top, 47 top, 51 bottom, 54 bottom, 56. DARROW M. WATT: pages 12 bottom right, 13 top and bottom, 64 right, 69 left and right, 74, 75, 76, 79 right. R. WENKAM: pages 25 top, 46 bottom left. WESTINGHOUSE ELECTRIC CORPORATION: pages 11 bottom, 20, 21 top and bottom, 22, 65, 66 left.